M000208467

HOW TO
STOP
PROCRASTINATING

A SIMPLE GUIDE TO
MASTERING DIFFICULT TASKS

STEVE SCOTT

How to Stop Procrastinating © 2017 by Oldtown Publishing LLC

All rights reserved. No part of this book may be reproduced in any form without permission in writing from the author. Reviewers may quote brief passages in reviews.

ISBN-13: 978-1-946159-12-0

Disclaimer

No part of this publication may be reproduced or transmitted in any form or by any means, mechanical or electronic, including photocopying or recording, or by any information storage and retrieval system, or transmitted by email without permission in writing from the publisher.

While all attempts have been made to verify the information provided in this publication, neither the author nor the publisher assumes any responsibility for errors, omissions, or contrary interpretations of the subject matter herein.

This book is for entertainment purposes only. The views expressed are those of the author alone, and should not be taken as expert instruction or commands. The reader is responsible for his or her own actions.

Adherence to all applicable laws and regulations, including international, federal, state, and local governing professional licensing, business practices, advertising, and all other aspects of doing business in the US, Canada, or any other jurisdiction is the sole responsibility of the purchaser or reader.

Neither the author nor the publisher assumes any responsibility or liability whatsoever on the behalf of the purchaser or reader of these materials.

Any perceived slight of any individual or organization is purely unintentional.

CONTENTS

Step #6: Implement 14 Daily Practices to Overcome Procrastination **95**

Exercise #7: Implement 14 Daily Practices to Overcome Procrastination **124**

YOUR FREE GIFT

As a way of saying thanks for your purchase, I'm offering a free report that's exclusive to readers of *How to Stop Procrastinating*.

With the *How to Stop Procrastinating Quick Start Guide*, you'll discover a printable reference guide of all the exercises, action items and checklists you can use to implement the following framework. Everything you need to get started is included in the **PDF that's part of the free companion website**.

Grab the How to Stop Procrastinating Quick Start Guide
www.developgoodhabits.com/procrastination-website

JOIN THE DGH COMMUNITY

Looking to build your goal-specific habits? If so, then check out the Develop Good Habits (DGH) community at **www.HabitsGroup.com**.

This is an excellent group full of like-minded individuals who focus on getting results with their lives. Here you can discover simple strategies for building powerful habits, find accountability partners, and ask questions about your struggles. If you want to "level up" the results from this book, then this is the place to be.

Just go to **www.HabitsGroup.com** to join the DGH Community.

INTRODUCTION

The following book *might* save your life.

Pretty crazy claim, right?

But hear me out: if you pay close attention to the words you're about to read and *implement* the strategies that I recommend, then this information could have a major impact on your life. It could help you prevent personal catastrophe.

How can I say this with 100% certainty?

Well, it relates to a simple word that has hundreds of meanings (depending on who you talk to).

That word is *procrastination.*

We all have a basic understanding of what this word means. Look it up in a dictionary and you'll see a definition like this one from Dictionary.com: "The act or habit of putting off or delaying, especially something requiring immediate attention."

But *how* we procrastinate and *what* we procrastinate on differs from person to person:

» A student will procrastinate in school, waiting until the last minute to study for a test or write a term paper.

» A professional will procrastinate on a work-related task

because it's challenging and requires hard work.

» And an athlete might procrastinate on getting an injury checked out because he or she doesn't want to miss an important game.

We all have personal reasons for procrastinating. And it's easy to fall into the trap of thinking it's not a big deal. You might even say to yourself: "It's just a bad habit that I have, but it's not that big of a deal."

The truth is that procrastination can have a serious effect on your life. It could even create a life-or-death situation. For instance, let's say you're experiencing pain and discomfort in your chest. Nine times out of ten, it *might be* nothing. But there's a small chance that it's a warning sign of an impending heart attack.

Unfortunately, some people will ignore (i.e., procrastinate on) a symptom like this and will die because of their failure to act. If only they had gone to the doctor the moment they experienced this warning sign, their life could have been saved.

Don't believe this happens?

Well, let me tell you a quick story to illustrate this point.

The Day My Father Almost Died

In 2007, I was in Virginia with my family visiting my aunt and cousin. On the day we were ready to drive home, my father complained of a painful discomfort in his chest.

He said something like: "I'll *probably* make an appointment this week with my doctor and get it checked out."

My response was the typical sarcastic comment you'd get in my family: "Yes, dad, that sounds like a *great plan*. I'm sure nothing bad will happen with your heart in the next five days. Or maybe you could go to the emergency room right away and make sure it's nothing serious."

At first, my dad blew off this comment.

But on the drive back, he thought about what I said and realized that maybe, just maybe, I had a valid point. So, he scheduled an emergency appointment with his doctor to make sure everything was okay with his heart.

The prognosis?

My dad required an immediate quadruple bypass heart surgery.

In fact, the doctor told my dad that if he waited even a *few* more days, he might have had a fatal heart attack.

Let me say it another way: If my dad *procrastinated* on an obvious heart issue, he would be dead right now. Fast-forward ten years; my dad is still an important part of my life. I see him twice a month when we go to the movies, have dinner together, and grab a few beers. He's also someone I turn to whenever I have a complicated business question. And he was there to see the birth of my son, Eugene, who also happens to be his namesake.

Now, I'm not sharing this story to brag about how I saved my dad's life. Honestly, I don't remember even making that sarcastic comment. (It's something that he reminded me of years later.) The purpose behind sharing this story is to illustrate how the smallest choices we make can often have the biggest impact on our lives. My dad is still here ten years after that warning sign because he chose to *not* procrastinate. I'm sure he was terrified at what the doctor might tell him, but he faced this issue head on by taking immediate action.

So, yes, the procrastination habit might *seem* like a small thing. But in the wrong scenario, it can have a massive—even lethal—impact on your life.

What Is Procrastination?

Now, before we move on, let's briefly talk about how I define procrastination and how it can negatively affect your life.

As I said before, procrastination can be defined as "the act or habit of putting off or delaying, especially something requiring immediate attention." But there's a lot more to that definition. Procrastination can lead to:

- » bad grades;
- » poor job performance;
- » unhealthy diet choices;
- » health issues;
- » financial problems.

Simply put: If you're someone who procrastinates, then this bad habit is limiting your success in a variety of ways. If you don't address this issue, then you'll reduce the likelihood that you'll achieve your major goals.

That's why it's critical that you focus on eliminating your procrastination tendencies by building what I call the "anti-procrastination habit."

Whether you're someone who lets the occasional task slip through the cracks or you always do things at the last minute, you'll discover an abundance of actionable advice in the following blueprint that's appropriately titled *How to Stop Procrastinating: A Simple Guide to Mastering Difficult Tasks*.

About *How to Stop Procrastinating*

This book is a straightforward, systematic framework for building an action-oriented habit throughout all the areas of your life. It's a breezy read, full of strategies that you can immediately implement in your life.

That said, this book also requires a bit of effort on *your* part. Not only do I expect you to read the material but I also want you to complete each of the exercises provided at the end of each step. I realize this is a big request to ask of someone who struggles with procrastination. That's why I've simplified each exercise, so it'll only require 30–60 minutes of your time.

You will learn a variety of things in *How to Stop Procrastinating*, like how to:

> » clarify all your professional tasks to understand why you're choosing to do each activity;

> » manage those day-to-day emergencies that pop up, which often can feel stressful and overwhelming;

> » evaluate all the opportunities that come your way and decide if they are worth pursuing (my philosophy is it's easy to not procrastinate if you never agree to do a task in the first place);

» prioritize your life so that you focus on what truly matters and "let go" of everything else;

» complete that challenging task (even when it's something you've been dreading);

» find that elusive work-life balance where you're able to work hard, play hard, and spend all those extra moments with people who enrich your life.

What you'll discover in *How to Stop Procrastinating* is a simple approach to managing all that comes into your life without feeling overwhelmed. You'll learn how to laser-focus on *your* priorities, respond appropriately to those emergencies, and permanently eliminate everything else (instead of procrastinating on them).

Finally, no author writes a book in isolation. Like you, I love reading books about productivity and personal development. So, whenever I discover a great strategy from someone else, I love sharing it with my readers.

That's why you'll discover that I often reference concepts that were previously covered in great books and websites, like *Getting Things Done, Eat That Frog, The ONE Thing, Essentialism, Deep Work, Zen Habits*, and James Clear.

While I do my best to provide the "golden nuggets" from these resources, I encourage you to check out each of them because they provide a more detailed explanation on some of the material covered in *How to Stop Procrastinating*.

About the Author

Before getting started, let me introduce myself and provide a little context about my belief on procrastination.

My name is Steve "S.J." Scott. I run the blog *Develop Good Habits*, and I'm the author of a series of habit-related titles, all of which are available at HabitBooks.com.

The purpose of my content is to show how continuous habit development can lead to a better life. Instead of lecturing you, I provide simple strategies that are easy to use, no matter how busy you get during the day.

Like many folks, my interest in procrastination started with a personal challenge that I had to overcome.

You see, for many years, I was what I like to call a "functional procrastinator." I was great at achieving long-term goals (like writing books, managing multiple internet businesses, and running marathons). On the other hand, I was *terrible* at following up on many of the day-to-day issues that didn't seem urgent, like getting the oil changed in my car, doing my taxes, or even grocery shopping.

The result was that I often let important priorities slip through the cracks because I thought I was "too busy" to do them.

My excuse was the standard line, pulled straight from the procrastinator's playbook: "I will get to them *someday*."

And, as you have probably guessed, "someday" almost never happened. I would go through life focusing on my long-term goals while allowing important issues to pile up on my desk.

The big wake-up call came from what I call "My $2,348.97 Mistake."

Like many procrastinators, I always filed for an extension on my taxes every year. Sometimes I prepaid some of the money, while other times I waited until the last minute, paying what my CPA calls a "stupidity tax."

Well, one year I filed my typical extension on my personal taxes, but I forgot to do the same thing for my business. After eventually filing in October of that year, I received a nice letter from the Internal Revenue Service that talked about my failure to file an extension for my business taxes. With interest and penalties, the letter stated that I owed the US government exactly $2,348.97—in addition to the money that I already paid for the year.

Sure, I could argue about the unfairness of the US taxation system. But the harsh reality is that I was $2,348.97 poorer because I procrastinated on a task that would have required only a single day of effort. In fact, even if I took an extra five minutes to fill out the extension for my business, I would have paid only a fraction of the interest and penalties.

After making that expensive mistake, I vowed to myself that I'd never let something stupid like that slip through the cracks. I swore that if something important popped up, I'd take care of it right way, without delay. And I promised myself that I would create a framework for my personal life where I would create that perfect balance between the important long-term goals with the urgent day-to-day stuff that we all deal with.

That system I created is what you're about to learn in *How to Stop Procrastinating*.

Now, let's get started by talking about why many people procrastinate.

8 REASONS WHY PEOPLE PROCRASTINATE

One reason overcoming procrastination can be a challenge is everyone has a different reason for doing it. What's more, the same person may have different reasons for putting off the various tasks in their life.

For example, maybe you feel too tired to call back your mother, telling yourself, "I can call her later this week." Or maybe you put off starting a new hobby because you're afraid of making a bunch of mistakes. Or you might procrastinate on a major project because you're secretly worried that it'll be a complete failure.

Simply put, beating procrastination is tough because we all have personal, but different, reasons for why we struggle with it. That said, if you want to break this bad habit, then you need to understand the common reasons why it happens and address this issue.

In this section, I'll review eight reasons why people procrastinate.

My suggestion?

Carefully read each one and ask yourself if it sounds like an excuse that you say to yourself whenever you want to put off a task.

Reason #1: You Are a Perfectionist

It's easy to procrastinate when you're worried about making a mistake that will expose a weakness. The fear of making mistakes is real, and it can cause people to put off some of their important obligations for another day.

This type of mindset is addressed in Carol Dweck's *Mindset: The New Psychology of Success*. In this book, Dweck relates successes in school, sports, work, the arts, and other areas of human endeavor to how one thinks about their talents and abilities.

Dweck explains that people have either a fixed mindset *or* a growth mindset.

Those with a fixed mindset believe that their abilities are set in stone, so they focus only on their current intelligence or talents, believing they can't be developed. They believe that they were born with what they have and they can't improve on their abilities. People with a fixed mindset also believe that effort is not needed if someone has talent. They believe talent just comes naturally.

So, why can a fixed mindset be dangerous? Because it hinders your ability to grow, learn, and make positive changes.

Alternatively, a growth mindset allows a person to believe their abilities can prosper and be developed through hard work. They believe that people's brains and talents are a mere starting point. They are born with their individual strengths, but there is *no limit* as to what can be accomplished. The growth mindset creates a desire to learn and an ability to overcome problems in order to be successful.

Dweck explains that mindset reveals how great teachers, parents, and managers can advance in their careers and achieve great accomplishments. With the correct mindset, people can motivate, lead, and teach in a way that can positively change their lives and the lives of others.

According to Hillary Rettig, the author of *The 7 Secrets of the Prolific: The Definitive Guide to Overcoming Procrastination, Perfectionism and Writer's Block*, people who procrastinate due to perfectionism tend to have a fixed mindset. This means that they avoid doing certain tasks because they fear the risk of making a mistake and looking anything less than perfect. They want their work to be perfect and cling to the idea that they will inevitably fail if the task is not in line with their given talents, so it's best to set it aside for another time.

While some may think that being a perfectionist is a positive trait, it's a quality that can have a long-term, detrimental repercussion on your success. It's a dangerous mix of antiproductive habits and attitudes that discourage progression. Although often misunderstood as having high standards, perfectionism limits the definition of success to an unrealistic standard.

Often, perfectionists will procrastinate because they fear that they will never achieve the high standard they set for themselves. They think: "Why should I even make the effort?"

Reason #2: You Fear the Unknown

Picture this: You notice one day a new mole that has appeared on your skin. You start to get anxious that it may be cancerous, so you avoid getting it checked out and secretly hope it'll go away on its own.

Does this sound like something you've done in the past?

Sometimes people are afraid of taking action because it may reveal a truth that they don't want to hear.

So, the old phrase "What you don't know can't hurt you" isn't true. In almost every case, if you ignore something for a long period of time, hoping it will go away, it will only get worse.

Researchers from the University of Michigan conducted a study on the effects of allowing misinformation to linger in someone's mind. The study notes that misinformation remains in an individual's memory and continues to influence their thinking, even if the person is aware that they are mistaken. The person is also likely to make use of the misinformation, especially if it fits with their existing beliefs and makes a logical story. This then leads to spreading the inaccurate information to other people.

This study applies to detriments in the environment, in politics, and at an individual level. Having misinformation or preconceived notions about health issues (such as "Cancer does not run in my family, so I am probably fine" or "The mole will go away with time") can end up doing significant damage.

The researchers found that your beliefs and personal views can be significant obstacles for changing believed misinformation. Additionally, an attempt to present someone with an unwanted truth that is against what they previously believed can even backfire and amplify their incorrect ideas. When it comes to personal health issues, ignoring the problem instead of facing the truth can certainly lead to a more severe issue and even death.

Think about it: What if the mole is a form of cancer that is completely treatable during the early stages but can grow malignant if it's ignored?

You could be proactive in getting the mole checked out and it would be an easy fix, or you could procrastinate because you want to assume everything is okay. In this case, what you don't know certainly can hurt you, and your personal belief that it will go away on its own is detrimental.

Some other examples of this phenomenon include avoiding going to the dentist and continuing to tell yourself that the cavity you suspect you have will be fine. Maybe you don't want to do your taxes because you're afraid to face the truth about how much money you owe the government. Perhaps you avoid a conversation with your spouse to delay the argument that it may cause.

This all ties back to the findings of the researchers at the University of Michigan because in these cases, the person doesn't want to know the truth. They are more comfortable with the possibility that everything is fine.

Ignorance is bliss, right?

The truth is that ignoring these situations can lead to grave circumstances.

The big lesson here: knowledge is power. Even if you receive bad news, the earlier you hear it, the more opportunities you will have to overcome a potentially worse situation.

As I learned from the cartoon *G.I. Joe* when I was a kid, "Knowing is half the battle!"

The earlier you can learn a harsh truth, the more time and opportunities you'll have to take corrective action if necessary.

So, ask yourself these important questions:

» What am I afraid of?

» What is the worst possible consequence that could happen?

» What could happen if I ignore the situation?

» Why am I putting this off?

» Is there *any* benefit to putting this off?

» How often do people die from avoiding a situation like this?

» Am I trying to convince myself of something that's not true?

» Am I scared of the process or the result?

» Can I handle the outcome?

» Am I trying to protect myself from a certain outcome?

» Am I actually scared or was I just told this was scary?

I'll admit that it's downright frightening to address tough issues, but there is almost never a good reason for putting off anything that can have a disastrous, negative impact on your life.

Reason #3: You Promise to Do It "Later"

This common excuse is a reminder that you can work on the pending task at some point in the future. It could be a few hours from now, in a couple of days, or the "perfect" free day that you envision sometime in the future.

Unfortunately, this line of thinking creates a strong disconnect between how you will *ideally* feel in the future and how you will *actually* feel in the future.

In your imagined future, you will have boundless energy, eat a healthy diet, exercise on a regular basis, and work well into the evenings in order to get everything finished.

However, the realistic "Future You" is tired, unmotivated, burned-out, handling unruly children, and craving chocolate cake.

This phenomenon relates to two concepts: the hot-cold empathy gap and time inconsistency. Let's start with the first concept and see how it relates to procrastination.

The Hot-Cold Empathy Gap

The hot-cold empathy gap is a concept that's widely covered in *Willpower* by Roy F. Baumeister and John Tierney. It's a state of mind that causes people to underestimate the influence of their instinctive drives on their attitudes, behaviors, and preferences.

The most important aspect of the hot-cold empathy gap is that human understanding greatly depends on one's state of mind. For example, if you're feeling angry, it's hard to picture yourself feeling calm. Or if you're hungry, it's hard to think of yourself as being full.

The inability to minimize the empathy gap can cause negative outcomes in professional settings. For example, when a doctor is gauging the physical pain of their patient or an employer is assessing how much paid leave an employee should get for a death in the family, these subjective decisions can easily be influenced by the hot-cold empathy gap. Maybe the doctor had previously been in a similar accident as the patient and feels like they are overreacting to their pain, or maybe an employer also recently had a death in the family but was able to return to work relatively quickly. These past experiences and feelings can have an influence on people's decisions.

Time Inconsistency

Time inconsistency is a situation where the decision-maker's preferences vary over time and their preferences become inconsistent. This mirrors the idea that there are different versions of yourself when making a decision. Each "self" represents the decision-maker at a certain point in time and the inconsistency happens when their preferences are not aligned.

For example, a study by Andersen et al. examined the decisions and actions of students. The night before an exam, many students wished they had one more day to study. If they were asked that night, some might agree to pay $10 for the exam to be postponed just one more day.

Alternatively, if asked months before the exam date, the students generally didn't feel the need to put the exam off. Consequently, most weren't willing to pay $10 to change the date of the exam.

While the choice is the same in both instances, it is made at different points in time. Because the decisions of the students change, they are exhibiting time inconsistency.

Another example of a time inconsistency was shown in a 1999 experiment published in the *Journal of Behavioral Decision Making*. In this study, subjects were offered a free movie rental. The movies fell into two categories: lowbrow entertainment (such as *Austin*

Powers) and highbrow entertainment (such as *Hamlet*).

Researchers analyzed the patterns of the choices that the subjects made. Without time inconsistency, you would expect that a subject would make the same choice regardless of when they made the decision versus when they were going to watch the movie. However, the decisions were different.

When subjects were asked to pick a movie to watch *right away*, most chose to watch a lowbrow movie. However, when they were faced with the decision of which movie to watch in four or more days, 70% of the subjects chose a highbrow movie.

What does this mean?

People's minds change over time, and the outcome of their decision in relation to the point in time that the decision is being made can certainly have a strong effect on how people think. People make different decisions for what will affect them in the immediate future rather than what will affect them down the road.

One interesting aspect of time inconsistency is the challenge of aligning the needs of Present You versus Future You.

James Clear, in his article titled "Two Harvard Professors Reveal One Reason Our Brains Love to Procrastinate," best describes this problem: "Future You knows you should do things that lead to the highest benefit in the long term, but Present You tends to overvalue things that lead to immediate benefit right now."

The average person spends too much time worrying about their Present Self, and not enough time thinking of how their actions can negatively influence their Future Self. It's easy to fall into the trap of not caring about the long-term costs of an action because the reaction will often happen in an undetermined amount of time.

Present You and Future You are constantly at odds. You might set a goal that you hope Future You will achieve, but it's always Present You who does the heavy lifting of working at this daily goal. And the only thing that Present You wants is to watch Netflix and eat a bag of potato chips.

To illustrate this point, think about an exercise goal you've made in the past. Odds are you imagined a Future You that exercises for an hour every day of the week and is full of energy. This version of you is fit and the envy of all your friends.

Unfortunately, Present You is tired from work and hungry for a snack. All you want to do is unwind after a long day. So, you skip the workout because the negative impact of not exercising isn't immediate. You then sit back and enjoy a relaxing evening because you simply don't want to work out.

This is a scenario that happens to people all the time. Future You has all sorts of dreams and plans, but Present You often succumbs to the instant gratification of an immediate reward.

Reason #4: You Focus on Easy Tasks

This probably sounds familiar: often you will choose to work on "filler" tasks because they are quick and easy to accomplish. This may include checking your email, talking to a coworker, or doing light paperwork.

While these tasks might give the appearance of "busyness" and make you believe that you're getting things done, they are a creative form of procrastination. Small tasks are easy to do and give you a quick sense of accomplishment, so by doing them first, you feel that rush of accomplishment and instant gratification.

The more time and effort it takes to do a task, the harder it is to get started. Without the instant dopamine rush from successfully finishing an activity, it's easy to push it off because the reward seems too far away. Many people want to feel successful and accomplished sooner rather than later.

All this relates to a concept called present bias. This term refers to a person's tendency to prioritize payoffs that are more immediate when considering the trade-offs between two future moments.

One study done at Princeton University studied subjects' brains while they made choices between immediate small rewards and larger rewards to be received at a later date.

Researchers found that there are two areas of the brain that compete for control over someone's behavior when they try to decide between near-term rewards and long-term goals. The researchers turned to a popular economic dilemma where consumers act impatiently in the present moment but plan to be patient in the future.

The study focused on 14 Princeton University students who were given a brain scan as they were asked to consider delayed-reward choices. One choice was a gift card to Amazon.com with values ranging from $5 to $40 at that moment or an unknown larger amount that the students could receive if they waited 2–6 weeks.

The researchers found that when subjects were considering choices involving the possibility of an immediate reward, parts of their brains influenced by emotional neural systems were activated. Additionally, all the decisions that were made, both short- and long-term, activated the brain systems associated with abstract reasoning.

Interestingly, when students had the option of getting a short-term reward but chose the more valuable delayed option, the calculating areas of their brains were more active than their emotional areas. When subjects chose the short-term reward, the activity of the two areas was similar, with a small swing toward more activity in the emotional area.

The study concluded that the option of short-term rewards activates the emotion-related area of the brain and overcomes the abstract-reasoning areas.

The researchers found that your emotional brain has a difficult time imagining the future, regardless of the fact that our logical brain can see the future consequences of current actions.

While our emotional brain wants to receive immediate pleasure, no matter the future damage, our logical brain knows to think about long-term effects. More often than not, the immediate hassle of having to wait for a payoff doesn't seem worth the unknown future benefits.

Reason #5: You Experience a Lack of Motivation

Have you ever thought to yourself that life *always* gets in the way of what you're supposed to do?

This lack of motivation can come from several underlying causes, including:

> » fatigue;
>
> » stress;
>
> » other priorities;
>
> » unexpected emergencies;
>
> » trouble formulating new ideas;
>
> » failures in the past with this task;
>
> » negativity from the people (and events) in your life;
>
> » lack of confidence;
>
> » working in the wrong environment; and
>
> » unclear goals.

You're not alone with feeling a lack of motivation for certain tasks. In a study done at Carnegie Melon University, it was revealed that people lack motivation when they find little value in the projected outcome of their work.

The lesson here is if you can connect a task to your interests, goals, and values, then you increase your motivation for working on it.

Reason #6: You Don't Know How to Get Started

What if the task at hand is too complex, unique, or difficult? What if it has a lot of moving parts, making it unclear where to begin? This uncertainty may keep you from starting because you don't know your first step.

Even if you can figure out the first step, once you are considering the process, it's easy to underestimate the time and commitment that's needed to complete a project.

The result is you'll often procrastinate on a task simply because you feel overwhelmed by all the steps that you're required to complete.

What's the best way to overcome this?

A very effective method is to use the approach David Allen discusses in his book *Getting Things Done*.

The idea here is to break down any multi-step project into a series of smaller tasks that can completed in a single block of effort. There are five steps to this process:

1. Write down the specific tasks that have your attention.
2. Decide which actions can be taken care of right away and do them.
3. Organize the rest of the task.
4. Constantly review your breakdown of tasks.
5. Do each task, one by one, until they are all finished.

You can even take these steps further by creating a checklist and getting the satisfaction of checking things off as you go. (We'll talk more about this concept in Step #3, where I show you how to break down any complex project.)

Reason #7: You Often Get Distracted

Let's dive into all the modern distractions that we're faced with daily:

- » Email messages.
- » Text messages.
- » Push notifications.
- » Social media updates.
- » Phone calls.
- » Meetings.
- » Skype calls.
- » People asking for your time.
- » Side tasks (e.g., errands, paperwork, desk organization).

The list goes on and on.

In fact, in a recent survey conducted by Career Builder, it was found that one in five employers believe that their workers spend fewer than five hours each day being productive. When looking for a reason for this, over half of the employers say that workers' smartphones are the first thing to blame, closely followed by spending time on the internet and gossiping around the workplace.

So, how can you keep these distractions at bay?

One simple solution is to design your environment so as to prevent those temptations from occurring in the first place. You can do this by:

» blocking the websites that often distract you using tools like SelfControl or Freedom;

» deleting games and apps on your smartphone;

» disabling wireless internet whenever you need to focus on deep work;

» putting your smartphone on airplane mode;

» wearing noise-canceling headphones;

» unplugging your router; and

» closing your door to avoid interruptions from coworkers or family.

Sure, some of these strategies might seem extreme. But they can be incredibly effective if you understand your temptations and are willing to remove them from your environment whenever you need to focus on an important task.

Reason #8: You Don't Have Enough Time

This is a common excuse for procrastination we've all given at one point. You have a task scheduled on your calendar, but life got in the way, so you're left only with a "little bit" of time to work on it. The amount of time is irrelevant. What's important is that in your mind, there's not enough time to complete a task, so you tell yourself that you'll do it later.

This excuse can take many forms: You don't have enough time to exercise. Or to work on a big project. Or to run the errands that you planned. Whenever you procrastinate on a task due to a lack of time, you're succumbing to the limiting belief that a little bit of effort doesn't make a difference.

There are two fixes for this form of procrastination. First, if you improve how you plan your schedule, you'll have enough time to complete the tasks that truly matter. Specifically, the one technique that I recommend is to do a daily and weekly review where you schedule blocks of time to work on the various activities in your life. This is something I'll cover at length in Step #5.

Next, *even* if you only have a few minutes to work on something, I recommend still doing something. The idea here is to use those "short slivers of time," as discussed by Suzanne Perez Tobias, that we all have to make a little bit of progress with your goals. Yes, you won't get the full "dosage" of hours spent on this activity, but something is better than nothing, right?

Consider these true-to-life examples:

> » *Don't have time for a full workout?* Then take a brisk 10- to 15-minute walk.

> » *Can't complete all the tasks on your to-do list?* Then pick the one that has the biggest long-term influence on your career and do that first.

> » *Don't have time to work on a report?* Then outline and map out what you'll write when you do have time.

> » *Can't run all your errands?* Then complete the most important one on your list.

» *Woke up late and can't complete your morning routine?* Then focus on the one or two healthy habits that give you energy for the rest of the day.

It's easy to feel frustrated when there's not enough time to complete all the tasks on your to-do list. But if you commit yourself to taking a little bit of action in the time that you do have, then at least you know that you didn't completely procrastinate on a task.

Exercise #1: Identify Your Procrastination Reasons

(Side note: This exercise and all the others are included in a downloadable "Quick Start Checklist" that's part of the companion website, which can be found here: www.developgoodhabits.com/procrastination-website.)

At the start of this chapter, I mentioned how we all have different reasons for procrastinating. When you identify *your* reasons, you'll take that first step to breaking this bad habit.

To begin, I recommend setting aside 30 minutes today to mull over the tasks you've procrastinated on within the past week or month. If you can't remember any examples, then do this exercise during the next week while you make decisions about your daily tasks.

First, write down each of the tasks, projects, or habits you've procrastinated on. The size or scope of the activity doesn't matter. The only requirement is that you've delayed taking action on it for some reason.

Next, write down the reason that you gave for putting it off. Be honest here, because this is for your eyes only. So, if you skipped a workout because you wanted to binge-watch season five of *House of Cards*, then write that reason down. Do this for all the activities that you've procrastinated on recently.

Third, look at the reasons you gave and see if they compare to the eight that I just detailed. Here they are again if you get stuck:

1. You are a perfectionist.

2. You fear the unknown.

3. You promise to do it "later."

4. You focus on easy tasks.

5. You experience a lack of motivation.

6. You don't know how to get started.

7. You often get distracted.

8. You don't have enough time.

Don't worry if your answers vary from task to task. Some activities you'll put off because you want them to be perfect. And other activities you'll procrastinate on because you weren't in the mood to do them. What's important is to understand the common reasons you give for putting off a task.

Finally, keep these reasons in the back of your mind as you read the rest of this book. Whenever you come across an idea that specifically addresses an issue that you have, highlight it and bookmark it for future use. Odds are this will lead to that breakthrough strategy whenever that issue pops up again in the future.

STEP #1: IDENTIFY YOUR
CURRENT COMMITMENTS

One challenge of modern living is that it's easy to let your to-do list snowball into numerous tasks, projects, and obligations. For some folks, it's impossible to complete every item on this list, which often causes that stressful feeling of overwhelm. You might even reach the point where you think it's impossible to get out of the massive hole that you've dug for yourself.

But don't worry if that sounds like you.

If you make a commitment to follow the advice that I've outlined in *How to Stop Procrastinating*, then you'll remove much of the anxiety and stress that comes from having too many tasks on your to-do list. Plus, you'll learn how to build a solid framework that prevents you from procrastinating on future activities.

To get started, I recommend a simple exercise that can take anywhere from 30–60 minutes. In the same notebook that you used in the previous exercise, write down *all* your current commitments and any goals you'd like to accomplish within the next year.

You can pick one of two options for completing this task:

1. The Getting Things Done (GTD) method.
2. How to Stop Procrastinating method.

Let me briefly go over each one.

Option #1: The Getting Things Done (GTD) Method

Detailed in one of the classic books on productivity, the GTD method rests on the idea of moving planned tasks and projects out of the mind by recording them externally and then breaking them into actionable work items. This allows one to focus attention on taking action on tasks instead of recalling them.

I'll be the first to admit that the GTD method is a vastly superior strategy for identifying all the "stuff" in your life. With this approach, you will gather 100% of all your incompletes. This includes any personal task, professional task, long-term goal, and random idea that you've ever had. This includes items like:

» current projects;

» bucket lists and "someday" goals;

» appointments;

» routine checkups (e.g., dental, medical, and appointments for your children);

» financial investments;

» commitments to others;

» responses to email messages and phone calls; and

» household chores or repairs.

These are just few examples. If you want to get the full picture of all that's included in the GTD method, then check out the full list that's provided courtesy of the site 43 Folders.

Again, I highly recommend the GTD approach because it's the most thorough method for identifying all the "open loops" in your life that require an action. That's why you might be interested in checking out David Allen's book *Getting Things Done* to complete this step of the process.

That said, I will say the following with as much humility as possible. The GTD approach is not for everybody—especially for people who already struggle with procrastination.

The time requirement for completing this life review *can take at least a day or two of focused effort*. It also requires a specific organizational structure for files and the stuff in your life. If you're someone who struggles to keep up with your day-to-day tasks, then you might find yourself overwhelmed by the GTD process.

That's why I'd like to offer an alternative solution in the paragraphs that follow.

Option #2: How to Stop Procrastinating Method

The exercise that I recommend for readers of this book is to think about everything that you must (or would like to) do for the next 3–12 months. Forget about your long-term goals or bucket list items. Just focus on the items that you have the ability and capacity to do from today until one year from now. That's it!

In the notebook that you started using during the previous exercise, write down the answers to these questions:

» Is there a medical issue that you've been putting off?

» What work-related projects are coming up?

» What personal projects are coming up?

» Is there a vacation that you'd like plan with your family?

» What habits would you like to build?

» Are there incomplete household tasks that you keep putting off?

» What meetings and appointments are coming up?

» What goals would you like to accomplish?

» Are there any important events coming up for your family members?

» Is there an exercise program you'd like to start?

» Are there any projects that you know you need to do but you've been putting off?

» Do you keep ignoring important—but not urgent—daily tasks?

You don't need to answer all these questions. In fact, you could ignore these prompts and write down whatever pops into your mind.

What's important here is to list all the unfinished items that have been going through your mind. These are the open loops that take up your mental bandwidth and cause you to feel anxious on a daily basis.

Finally, *where* you keep this list doesn't really matter. It could be in a notebook like I suggested in the previous step or in an app like Evernote. The important thing is to store all these tasks in a central place that you'll have access to every day, because you'll be referring to this list throughout the rest of the steps in this book.

Exercise #2: Write Down All Your Current Commitments

To recap, I suggest a simple, three-step exercise that will require about 30–60 minutes of your time:

1. In a notebook (or an app like Evernote), write down all your current commitments and any activities you'd like to do within the next year.

2. Focus on the immediate future by using these prompts:

    ◦ Is there a medical issue that you've been putting off?

    ◦ What work-related projects are coming up?

    ◦ What personal projects are coming up?

    ◦ Is there a vacation that you'd like plan with your family?

    ◦ What habits would you like to build?

    ◦ Are there incomplete household tasks that you keep putting off?

    ◦ What meetings and appointments are coming up?

    ◦ What goals would you like to accomplish?

    ◦ Are there any important events coming up for your family members?

    ◦ Is there an exercise program you'd like to start?

    ◦ Are there any projects that you know you need to do but you've been putting off?

- ○ Do you keep ignoring important—but not urgent—daily tasks?

3. Keep this list handy as you work your way through the rest of the exercises provided in this book.

STEP #2: FOCUS ON FIVE CORE PROJECTS

Let me start this section with a short disclaimer: what you're about to read will be the most mentally challenging step in the entire book. The recommended exercise isn't hard to do. But staying committed to it will require a level of dedication that most people don't possess. That said, I guarantee if you stay the course, this framework will become your secret weapon to *permanently* eliminating your procrastination habit.

The typical advice you learn from *most* time-management books is learning how to cram as many tasks into your schedule as possible. I feel this advice is one of the reasons why many people procrastinate. Their lives are filled with so many tasks and obligations that they simply don't have time to do them all.

In our modern society, it seems like many folks wear their overworked, overbooked, frenetic schedule like a badge of honor. It's no longer about *what* you produce, but how many hours you've worked each week. Just look on social media and you'll see lots of humblebrag updates that end with *#hustle*.

On the other hand, if you study the most successful people in the world, you'll see that they don't juggle dozens of projects. Instead, they identify what they're good at and double down on the handful activities related to what author Gary Keller calls "The ONE Thing" in his book by the same name.

My point? It's easy to procrastinate if your daily to-do list is filled with dozens of tasks and projects. You'll feel so overwhelmed that you can't help but put off many activities. And often the tasks that you procrastinate on are the ones that can have a massive, positive impact on your life.

So how do you fix this?

It's simple: narrow down your attention to just a handful of core projects. As we've discussed, people often procrastinate because they feel overwhelmed by all their obligations. But if you limit your focus to only a few options, then it's easy to take consistent, productive action. The best example of this strategy is called the 25–5 Rule.

The 25–5 Rule Explained

The 25–5 Rule is a concept that I learned from the Live Your Legend site, where Scott Dinsmore shared a story titled "Warren Buffett's 5-Step Process for Prioritizing True Success (and Why Most People Never Do It)" about meeting a friend of Warren Buffett's pilot (whom he calls Steve).

In this conversation with Dinsmore, Steve talked about how Buffett encouraged him to write down a list of 25 things he wanted to do over the next few years. After completing this list, Buffett told him to review this list and circle his top five priorities. These goals would be more important than anything else in Steve's life.

Next, Buffett encouraged Steve to create an action plan for these five activities. Buffett instructed him to write them down as actionable goals and get started on them immediately.

Toward the end of this conversation, Buffett asked a simple question: "But what about these other 20 things on your list that you didn't circle? What is your plan for completing those?"

Steve's reply was probably what most of us would say: "Well, the top five are my primary focus, but the other twenty come in at a close second. They are still important, so I'll work on those intermittently as I see fit as I'm getting through my top five. They are not as urgent, but I still plan to give them dedicated effort."

Buffett's reply was surprising: "No. You've got it wrong, Steve. Everything you didn't circle just became your 'avoid at all costs' list. No matter what, these things get no attention from you until you've succeeded with your top five."

Great advice, right?

Well, I can tell you that the 25–5 Rule *really* works when you apply it in the real world. In fact, I've been following it for over a year and it's had an amazing effect on my life—specifically when it comes to preventing procrastination.

After making the commitment to focus only on five things at a time, I've had more business success and personal happiness than I did when my life was filled with dozens of weekly projects, obligations, appointments, and piles of "someday" tasks.

As an example, my *current* five focuses (in order of priority) are:

1. being present with friends and family;

2. completing an IRONMAN race;

3. writing and marketing my books;

4. increasing web traffic to my blog, DevelopGoodHabits.com, and converting these visitors into email subscribers;

5. fixing and updating sections of my home.

What's powerful about the five-project focus is it's easy to make decisions about my daily tasks. Each day, I review the items on my Todoist app and any new requests for my time. If the activity *doesn't* match one of these five goals, then I immediately say no (which is a concept that we'll talk more about in Step #4).

Now, it's not written in stone that you concentrate only on five projects. You could have a few more or a few less. The important thing is to proactively think about your time, commitments, and where you spend the most time. If every one of your actions is directly aligned with a goal, then you'll feel excited to do it, which is the ultimate procrastination killer.

So how do you identify these five projects?

Well, the first step is to examine your core values. If you match your internal beliefs to your current obligations, then it's not hard to exclusively focus on the activities that make you happy. So, let's talk about that next.

How to Identify Your Core Values

Your core values directly relate to your belief system. These values often guide your behavior and state of mind to create your own personal set of rules. By honoring these values, you will reduce your stress when it comes to the tasks that you often procrastinate on.

Most people live a life that's filled with more work than they can possibly get done. Add the demands of exercise, family, a social life, religious services and worship, hobbies, and civic duties and it becomes impossible to do everything.

For me, I know that my most important value is spending time with my wife, son, extended family, and friends. To put it simply, my focus of being present with the people in my life is the top core value on which I base every other decision. If an activity directly conflicts with this rule (and can't be rescheduled), then I will refuse to do it.

Unfortunately, most people aren't truly aware of their own core values. Rather than thinking about what is important to us, we tend to focus on the values of our culture, society, and what the media tells us is important.

While it may be simple to speculate what your values should be, knowing and accepting your core values takes a lot of thought and effort. Here are seven actions that will help you identify your core values.

Action #1: Get In the Right State of Mind

Take time to empty your mind of any outside influences. Perhaps you were recently with friends who made it clear what their values were, or maybe it is Sunday and you have just left a church event.

The point here is our decisions are often skewed by the values that other people want us to believe. So, to identify *your* core values, try to erase all the programming in your mind that comes from other people and start with a fresh outlook on what you want.

Action #2: Reflect On the Times in Your Life When You Were the Happiest

Consider times from both your professional and your personal life to make sure you have balanced thoughts.

When you think about being happy in the past, what were you doing? Were you with anybody in particular? Were there any other factors that were contributing to your state of happiness?

Picture in your mind those moments when you truly felt fulfilled—those are the values that you should build on.

Action #3: Think of a Time When You Were Proud of Yourself

Again, think about your personal and your professional life.

Has there been a point in your life where you have felt especially proud or confident in yourself? What caused that to happen? Was it a great personal accomplishment or maybe something that allowed you to share your pride with other people? Who was involved?

Action #4: Identify What Has Made You Feel Fulfilled or Satisfied in the Past

Think about the voids that you have had in your life and how they have been filled.

When you have had your needs met, what about that particular experience added meaning to your life? Who was involved and how much outside involvement did they have to have? Were there other contributing factors? How and why did the experience give your life meaning?

Action #5: Determine Your Core Values Based on Your Past Experiences of Happiness, Pride, and Satisfaction

Think back on actions 2–4 and consider why each experience was positive and memorable. Did they all have a common factor? Is there something that is noticeably missing from all these experiences?

Action #6: Align These Experiences with Value Words

Your core values work to guide you and determine your behavior. In order to continue growing, you must identify your values on a regular basis and then work to make any necessary changes to your life so your actions and behavior are in line with your values.

Being true to your values helps to cultivate happiness, fulfillment, and success, because your beliefs come into line with your actions. You can reference my friend Barrie Davenport's list of value words to help get you started with finding the words that best describe what's important to you.

Some of these values include:

>> accomplishment;

>> control;

>> dependability;

>> camaraderie;

- » commitment;

- » enjoyment;

- » gratitude;

- » appreciation;

- » inspiration;

- » consistency;

- » belongingness;

- » philanthropy;

- » hopefulness;

- » fidelity;

- » discipline; and

- » creativity.

Action #7: Prioritize Your Important Values

This is an important step, yet it's perhaps the most difficult step in the process. In order to pick out your top values, visualize a situation where you would have to choose between two values. For example, if you compare your core values of philanthropy and belongingness, ask this question: What if you had to decide whether to move to a foreign country to do valuable aid work or remain in your hometown and volunteer and do local charity work? Go through your list of values with this in mind to home in on your core values.

Repeat this process until you've identified the values that directly relate to the potential projects. Once you have these in mind, you'll make more effective decisions about the five core projects that you'll select.

How to Select Your Five Core Projects

It's my hope that the biggest lesson you'll get from this book is accepting the fact that you have only a limited amount of time each week. Would you rather spend your time stressing over dozens of different obligations or would you like to focus on a handful of core activities that truly enrich your life?

Hopefully you picked the first option!

If so, then I recommend another exercise that takes three steps to complete.

First, write down (at least) 25 projects or activities that you might focus on. How you define *projects* is up to you. But generally speaking, I consider a project to be anything that requires at least an hour or two of my time each week. This can include:

> » coaching your kid's soccer team;
> » starting a side business;
> » working out;
> » learning a new skill;
> » going to school;
> » tackling work-related projects;
> » planning a trip;
> » buying a new house; and
> » dating and/or being in a relationship.

Now, I'll admit that it might be weird to label some of these actions as projects—especially the part about dating and relationships.

Not very romantic, right?

But look at this way: if your schedule is filled with too many tasks and projects, then I guarantee you're probably not being present in your relationships. In my opinion, if you want to build something that lasts, then it needs to be a priority.

To get started on this first step, I recommend writing down every possible goal and outcome you'd like to focus on in the next year. Don't be afraid to jot down anything that pops into your mind, because you might discover something that truly matters to you.

Second, take 30–60 minutes to examine this list and narrow down your focus to five projects. One way to do this is to match each item to the core values that came up in the previous exercise. Ask yourself, "Which option do I feel most excited to focus on for the next few months?" Also be sure to account for the areas of your life where there would be a serious consequence if you ignored it (like your job).

Ultimately, what you choose should be a good balance of your personal obligations with one or two projects that make you feel excited.

Third, commit to focusing *only* on these five items for the next few months. This means that you'll have to *purposefully* procrastinate on many projects that sound interesting but that you don't have time for. Yes, this will require a bit of willpower (and frequently saying no), but you'll discover that when you singularly focus on a handful of activities, it's easier to get things done and avoid the trap of procrastination.

Now, it's not enough to focus on five projects at a time. If you don't know *what outcomes* you'd like to accomplish, then you'll still end up procrastinating. That's why I recommend creating S.M.A.R.T. goals, which we'll talk about in the next step.

Exercise #3: Focus on Five Core Projects

One of the simplest ways to overcome procrastination is to narrow your attention by focusing on a handful of projects. The method that I recommend is the 25–5 Rule. With this strategy, you'll list 25 projects or areas of your life that sound compelling, identify five that you want to focus on, and make a commitment to completely ignore everything else.

To figure out where to direct your attention, I suggest completing a seven-step exercise to identify the values in your life:

1. Get in the right state of mind by challenging every belief that comes from an outside source. If you feel that a thought has been influenced by someone else (parents, friends, religious institutions, media, and so on), then take a few minutes to reexamine your thoughts to see if they are something that you truly believe in.

2. Reflect on the times in your life when you were the happiest. Ask yourself, "What was I doing? Who was I with? Why did I feel happy?"

3. Think of the times when you were proud of yourself. What did you accomplish? How did that achievement make you feel? What was it about this activity that made you feel fulfilled?

4. Identify what has made you feel fulfilled or satisfied in the past. How and why did the experience give your life meaning?

5. Determine your core values based on your past experiences of happiness, pride, and satisfaction. Review the previous steps and identify the common elements of these peak moments.

6. Align these experiences with value words like *accomplishment, enjoyment, philanthropy*, and *creativity*.

7. Prioritize these values in order of importance.

After you've identified your values, complete another 30- to 60-minute exercise where you identify your five core projects:

» Write down (at least) 25 projects or activities you could focus on.

» Take 30 minutes to examine this list and narrow down your focus to only five projects.

» Commit to focus *only* on these five items for the next few months.

STEP #3: SET QUARTERLY S.M.A.R.T. GOALS

As we just discussed, a simple way to prevent procrastination is to focus *only* on activities that directly align with a handful of goals. This works because whenever you feel that urge to put off a task, you can remind yourself of how your inaction negatively affects an outcome that you desire in the immediate future.

When it comes to goal setting, my suggestion is to set S.M.A.R.T. goals for every quarter (i.e., three months) instead of the yearlong goals that most people create.

To begin, let's start with a simple definition of S.M.A.R.T. goals.

George Doran first used the S.M.A.R.T. acronym in the November 1981 issue of the *Management Review*. It stands for:

> » Specific;
>
> » Measurable;
>
> » Attainable;
>
> » Relevant; and
>
> » Time-bound.

Specific

Specific goals answer your six "W" questions: "Who?", "What?", "Where?", "When?", "Which?", and "Why?"

When you can identify each element, you'll know which tools (and actions) are required to reach a goal:

- » Who is involved?
- » What do you want to accomplish?
- » Where will you complete the goal?
- » When do you want to do it?
- » Which requirements and constraints might get in your way?
- » Why are you doing it?

Specificity is important because when you reach these milestones (date, location, and objective), you'll know for certain you have achieved your goal.

Measurable

Measurable goals are defined with precise times, amounts, or other units—essentially anything that measures progress toward a goal.

Creating measurable goals makes it easy to determine if you have progressed from point A to point B. Measurable goals also help you figure out when you're headed in the right direction and when you're not. Generally, a measurable goal statement answers questions starting with *how*, such as "How much?", "How many?", and "How fast?"

Attainable

Attainable goals stretch the limits of what you think is possible. While they're not impossible to complete, they're often challenging and full of obstacles. The key to creating an attainable goal is to look at your current life and set an objective that seems *slightly* beyond your reach. That way, even if you fail, you still accomplish something of significance.

Relevant

Relevant goals focus on what you truly desire. They are the exact opposite of inconsistent or scattered goals. They are in harmony with everything that is important in your life, from success in your career to happiness with the people you love.

Time-Bound

Time-bound goals have specific deadlines. You are expected to achieve your desired outcome before a target date. Time-bound goals are challenging and grounding. You can set your target date for today, or you can set it for a few months, a few weeks, or a few years from now. The key to creating a time-bound goal is to set a deadline you'll meet by working backward and developing habits (more on this later).

> **Side note:** Okay, here's where it might get confusing. Sometimes the "three-month rule" doesn't apply for every situation. Occasionally you'll have a major goal that demands your attention, but doesn't neatly fit into a quarterly block of time.

For instance, one of my current goals is to complete an IRONMAN race, which is five months away as I'm writing this. Training for this race is still a critical part of my day, but I won't achieve the outcome until two months after the deadline of this quarter.

The point here is like everything else in this book, the three-month rule isn't written in stone. Use it as a general guideline—not as an absolute must.

Examples of S.M.A.R.T. Goals

A S.M.A.R.T. goal is clear and well-defined. There is no doubt about the result you want to achieve. At its deadline, you'll know if you *have* or *haven't* achieved a particular goal.

As an example, here are S.M.A.R.T. goals related to seven core values that many people have:

1. **Career**: "I will acquire five new projects for my web design consultancy through referrals, networking, and social media marketing campaigns within three months."

2. **Family**: "I will strengthen my bond with my family by taking them for a vacation at least once in six months. This will be accomplished by setting aside two hours each month to plan our family trip."

3. **Marriage**: "I will identify three things I really love about my partner and tell her about them on Friday night. This will be done by scheduling a 30-minute block on Tuesday so I can reminisce about all the good times we've shared together."

4. **Spirituality:** "I will take five minutes each day to give thanks for everything that's good in my life. I will develop this habit by setting aside time right before my lunch to remember what's important."

5. **Artistry:** "I will dedicate three hours every week to learn and practice watercolor painting. This will be done by eliminating unimportant habits, like watching TV."

6. **Finances:** "I will save 10 percent of every paycheck and invest it in index funds through Vanguard."

7. **Fitness:** "I will work out a minimum of 30 minutes per day, three days per week by December 31."

Hopefully, these seven examples give you an idea of how to create S.M.A.R.T. goals that lead to a balanced life. Now, let's go over a six-action process you can use to create your goals.

Action #1: Focus on Five Projects

As mentioned before, people often procrastinate because they say yes to everything, which causes them to feel overwhelmed by their laundry list of obligations. That's why I recommend focusing on just five projects, like I discussed in the previous section.

Not only will you make more progress with these five areas of your life, you'll also feel less stressed because you're not trying to juggle dozens of personal responsibilities.

Action #2: Focus on Three-Month Goals

It's been my experience that long-term goals constantly shift. What seems urgent today often isn't urgent next month. Lengthy goals (i.e., anything over six months) are often *demotivating*. When you know a deadline is months away, it's easy to procrastinate on a task today. The result is you'll put off a task, promising you'll work on it *next* week. Next thing you know, it's a year later and nothing has been accomplished.

You can fight your procrastination tendencies by taking the five priorities in your life and breaking them down into three-month S.M.A.R.T. goals.

As an example, let's talk again about my current five projects:

1. Being present with friends and family.
2. Completing an IRONMAN race.
3. Writing and marketing my books.
4. Increasing web traffic to my blog, DevelopGoodHabits.com, and converting these visitors into email subscribers.
5. Fixing and updating sections of my home.

These are the general outcomes that I'm currently focusing on, but most don't have a concrete outcome. So, they need to be turned into a series of S.M.A.R.T. goals that I hope to achieve by September 30, 2017. As you'll see, some of these are one-time milestones and others are specific habits that I'd like to incorporate into my day.

1. Being Present with Friends and Family

> » Shut down my laptop by 5:00 p.m. every evening.

> » Dedicate 7:00 a.m. to 11:00 a.m. every day to spending time with my son.

> » Go on a date with my wife at least once every two weeks.

> » Visit my parents at least once every two weeks.

> » Go on a week-long vacation with the entire family in Cape Cod, Massachusetts, in July 2017.

> » Go on a week-long vacation with my wife and son to the Finger Lakes in New York in August 2017.

2. Completing an IRONMAN Race

> » Build up to an average of 20 hours per week of combined exercise time.

> » Complete two or three 20-mile training runs.

> » Complete two or three 3-mile swims.

> » Complete one or two 100-mile bike rides.

> » Complete three short-distance triathlon races.

> » Complete a half-IRONMAN.

> » Complete IRONMAN Florida on November 4, 2017.

3. Writing and Marketing My Books

> » Write, publish, and launch three books (*How to Stop Procrastinating*, *Upgrade Your Lifestyle*, and a revised version of *Master Evernote*).

» Create an email follow-up sequence for each of these three books.

» Set up pay-per-click campaigns (through Amazon Marketing Services) for each of my five top-selling books.

4. Increasing Web Traffic to My Blog, DevelopGoodHabits.com, and Converting These Visitors into Email Subscribers

» Optimize the 50 most-visited web pages by targeting specific keywords to increase their traffic.

» Build an email marketing sequence for each of the ten top performing categories of content.

» Write and publish at least two articles per week.

5. Fixing and Updating Sections of My Home

» Finalize the organization of my home office.

» Set up a bat house in our garden (an article on WellnessMama.com explains the benefits).

» Repair at least ten items around my house.

Those are the important milestones from my list of five projects. As you can see, it's not hard to break down a priority into a series of specific goals, each with a specific deadline and action item.

Action #3: Use a Weekly Review to Tweak Your Goals

It's *not* always easy to consistently work on your goals when you have a dozen other obligations. Fortunately, there is a simple solution to this dilemma—schedule a weekly review session where you create a daily action plan for the next seven days.

The weekly review is important because life is always changing, which means you'll need to make small, constant adjustments to your schedule. And occasionally, you'll discover that you're no longer interested in one of your five core projects. So, you can also use the weekly review to switch your focus to something else.

The weekly review is a vital part of the anti-procrastination process, so we'll talk more about this concept in the section that I've devoted to planning your week.

Action #4: Turn Each Focus into a Project

Think back to the eight reasons that people procrastinate. One of the biggest roadblocks you'll face is not knowing how to get started with a task. When you have "write report" on your to-do list, it's easy to put it off because this action item doesn't have an obvious first step.

That's why you should turn any multi-step activity into a project—with tasks that can be completed in a short block of time.

The advantage of creating a project list is you never have to guess about your next action. Instead, you can use a key technique from *Getting Things Done* in which you continuously ask one question whenever you work on a project: "What's my next step?" Then, once you've identified this action, you make forward progress on one of your five core projects.

Yes, on the surface this might seem like simplistic advice. But I think it's a very effective strategy, because people often procrastinate on ambiguous tasks when they don't know the next step they need to take. For instance, the book you're currently reading required over a hundred separate actions to go from idea to publication. That's *in addition to* the habit of writing for 30–90 minutes every day. Here are just the first 12 steps that I have on my project list that I need to complete before I even write the first word:

1. Think of a basic book idea (look in my book "idea garden").

2. Go to Amazon to gauge the profit potential of a book idea; use the rule of #30,000 (described on Authority Pub) to see if it's popular topic.

3. Poll my audience to identify their specific challenges with this topic.

4. Create a folder for the book project on my desktop, in Evernote, and in Todoist.

5. Identify the hook and basic premise for the book.

6. Dedicate two weeks for brainstorming talking points.

7. Identify seven target keywords.

8. Research the topic, including reading books, reviewing Blinkist and using Google to find quality references.

9. Do a book "brain dump" to brainstorm every possible idea to include.

10. Review these notes by identifying potential chapters and fleshing them out.

11. Sort the index cards into a logical order.

12. Map the outline.

As you can see, this partial project list is a mixed bag of actions that take from a few minutes to a few hours of effort. But the critical thing to remember is to have a central hub for every project with clear actions for each step of the process. Done correctly, this project list will become an invaluable companion you'll refer to throughout the day.

It's not hard to create a project list. In fact, you can get started in five minutes with two great tools that are completely free—Todoist and Evernote.

Todoist and Evernote each have a specific benefit, so let me give you a brief overview of both, and then we'll talk about how they can be used to assist your efforts at maintaining the projects in your life.

Evernote is a cross-platform tool that allows you to take notes, capture ideas, and organize this information into a file structure that's based on your personal needs. You can use Evernote to create simple text-based notes, upload photos, record voice reminders, add videos, and clip specific web pages. Anything that can be digitized can be uploaded to Evernote.

I like Evernote because it can act as a central location to capture any important idea or thought: a strategy you'd like to implement, a website to bookmark, or a time marker for a multimedia file. Basically, whenever you come across a piece of information that's important for your long-term success, it should go into Evernote.

It's easy to get started with Evernote. My recommendation is to create a "notebook" for your skill and then add notes for each reminder or idea that pops into your head. An article on Evernote titled "Organize With Notebooks" can walk you through the entire process.

Todoist is the perfect tool for creating and managing project lists. I prefer this app over others, because it allows me to maintain multiple projects and store tasks for each one while also creating simple daily lists that don't cause me to feel overwhelmed.

Like Evernote, Todoist isn't difficult to use. Simply create a project for your skill, add tasks for that project, and then schedule these items into your weekly routine. To get started, the Todoist blog provides a quick start guide.

If you feel confused by either of these apps, I've created a simple video that walks you through each one. You can access these videos on the free companion website.

Action #5: Review Your Goals

The key to achieving anything in life is *consistency*. That's why you should review the list for each of the five projects and make sure you're hitting every important milestone. I recommend creating specific measurements for each step of the process and using a weekly review to make sure you're touching on those as well.

Setting aside time for a daily review is a key step to achieving any goal. It doesn't matter how busy you are—if you are not reviewing your goals every day, you will be less likely to succeed.

The truth is, sometimes life can throw major curve balls in your pursuit of a long-term objective. Often, these challenges can be frustrating and cause you to feel less excited about a goal. So, my advice is simple: review your goals *at least* two times per day. That way, you can keep them at the forefront of your mind and remind yourself why you're taking a specific action on a daily basis.

Action #6: Evaluate Your Quarterly Goals

You work hard on your goals every day. The problem? Some people never take a step back and understand the "why" behind each goal. In other words, people don't review their goals to see if they're *actually* worth pursuing. That's why it's important to evaluate your goals every three months, make sure they're aligned with your life purpose, and then create new goals based on what you've learned.

You can complete this evaluation by answering questions like:

» Have I attained the desired outcome?

» What were the successful *and* unsuccessful strategies?

» Did I put 100% of my effort toward completing these goals? If not, why?

» Have I achieved results consistent with my efforts?

» Should I create a similar goal for the next quarter?

» What goals should I eliminate or alter?

» Is there anything new I'd like to try?

Even though it takes a few hours to complete this evaluation, you should take time to do it every quarter. It will be your ultimate safeguard against wasting time on a goal that *doesn't* align with your long-term plans.

Now, the best way to make sure you have enough time to work on these goals is to remove everything from your life that prevents you from taking action, which is what I'll cover in the next step.

Exercise #4: Set Your Quarterly S.M.A.R.T. Goals

We often procrastinate on tasks that don't provide instant gratification. However, if you attach each task to an immediate goal, you increase the odds that you'll be motivated enough to get started. The simplest way to do this is to set S.M.A.R.T. goals for every quarter (i.e., three months) instead of the yearlong goals that most people set.

S.M.A.R.T. stands for:

» **S**pecific;

» **M**easurable;

» **A**ttainable;

» **R**elevant; and

» **T**ime-bound.

You can create these quarterly goals by completing a simple six-action exercise:

1. Focus on five projects and commit to focusing only on these activities.

2. Create goals with an immediate deadline (I suggest every three months).

3. Use a weekly review to track and adjust your goals.

4. Turn each focus into a project by clearly identifying all the steps you need to complete.

5. Review your goals to remind yourself of the long-term benefit of taking action on the activities you might want to procrastinate on.

6. Evaluate your goals every quarter and use this feedback to make more effective goals for the next three months.

STEP #4: SAY NO TO COMPETING PROJECTS AND OBLIGATIONS

Saying no is another part of the anti-procrastination process that will be difficult to implement. Again, not because it's hard to do, but because it requires a deep level of commitment that most people don't have when it comes to their personal goals.

In this step, I'm asking you say no when it comes to *any* task, project, or obligation that doesn't perfectly align with the goals that you've set for yourself.

What does this have to do with procrastination? Well, there are three reasons why this step is an important part of the process.

First, by now you know that the feeling of overwhelm is often the biggest cause of procrastination. When you feel like you have too much to do daily, it's easy to push off the difficult stuff because you don't have the physical or mental bandwidth to do them well.

Second, it's also easy to fall into the trap of agreeing to the requests for your time from other people simply because you don't want to disappoint anyone. We all want to be liked, so we'll agree to something—even when we know it's something we don't have time to do.

Finally, it's easy to "tinker" on projects that sound fun, but aren't part of your five core projects. This is a dangerous practice, because whenever you say yes to something new, you're basically saying no to the projects that you've already identified as being important.

Just think back to the list of 25 items that you brainstormed in Step #2. While you picked 5 core projects, you also had to say no to the other 20. The problem here is that they are 20 items in which you have some personal interest. Unfortunately, on some level, they can be the biggest distraction of them all because you'll often feel the occasional urge (possibly induced by a bit of guilt) to focus on these activities.

For instance, when I did the 25–5 challenge, there were an additional 15 items that I included on my list. Each was a compelling project that I'd love to do, but when compared to the five that I selected, I chose to put them off:

1. Create a physical product.
2. Launch a podcast related to habits and personal development.
3. Create an information product related to habits and personal development.
4. Scale-up my existing product that teaches self-publishing.
5. Master Facebook ads.
6. Go on a "podcast tour" to promote my book *Habit Stacking*.
7. Start playing the trumpet (again).
8. Get into CrossFit®.
9. "Level up" my cooking and meal-preparation efforts.
10. Start gardening around my house.

11. Section-hike the Appalachian Trail.

12. Join more local Meetup groups and expand my social circle.

13. Learn to speak Spanish.

14. Improve my photography skills.

15. Join a local real estate investing club.

Sure, some of these ideas are farfetched—they are bucket list ideas that sound good, but I'm currently unsure of how they'll fit into my schedule. On the other hand, there are a few ideas that I would love to do now, but I recognize that time spent on them is time taken away from the five projects that are important to me.

So, by now you know it's important to say no to anything that conflicts with the core projects in your life.

The question is: "How do I say no without ticking people off or getting into trouble at work?"

Well, you can do this by building five practices into your routine.

Practice #1: Say No as Early and Politely as Possible

Be up-front with people about their requests. If you know you can't follow through on a task, then be firm and tell them right away.

Honesty really *is* the best policy here. Simply tell the person that you have a few priority projects that require your full attention and you can't afford the distraction. Usually, most people will understand the need to focus on the priority tasks.

Try to end the conversation on a positive note. If you can't help the person, recommend someone who can. If you know of a helpful resource, offer that as an alternative. And if you think that you *might* grant the request sometime in the future, then ask the person to follow up on a specific date.

Saying no doesn't make you a selfish person. It makes you someone who clearly understands what's important. By having clear goals, you don't allow the demands of others to distract you from completing important projects.

Practice #2: Identify the Mandatory Tasks

We all have obligations that aren't always fun but still need to be completed because they're a vital part of being a normal, well-adjusted adult. In other words, if you say no to every request for your time, you probably won't get very far in life.

We all have things that *must* be done, so you might as a well accept that you have to do things, no matter how much you don't like them.

My only advice is to relate each task to one of the five core projects that you've previously identified.

For instance, let's say you hate doing the dishes. It's an annoying task that eats into your schedule and sometimes you're too tired to worry about a few dishes in the sink. On the other hand, if being part of a harmonious marriage is an important goal, then you can view the dishes as an important part of the relationship because you're doing something that makes your spouse happy.

Now, don't worry if you find yourself procrastinating on these mandatory tasks. In Step #6, I will detail 14 practices on how to take consistent action—even when completing a specific task is something that you've been dreading.

Practice #3: Compare Each Request to Your Current Projects

As the German military strategist Helmuth von Moltke once said, "No battle plan survives contact with the enemy."

The lesson that *I* take from this quote is while it's easy to mentally commit to only five projects, it's a whole other challenge to stay the course when you discover new opportunities or receive requests for your time from the people in your life.

That's why I highly recommend taking a few minutes whenever there's a request for your time to compare it against your current priorities and projects.

You've already identified what's important to you, so when you get a request to do something, compare it to your desired outcomes. If they don't match, then have the courage to say no to the requester.

Here's a simple three-part process to quickly evaluate any request for your time:

1. **Compare the new opportunity to your current list of five projects.** Is there an existing project that's not as important as the new one? If so, ask yourself what the worst-case scenario would be if you removed it from your life or put it on hold.

2. **Figure out the reason why you might be interested in replacing one of your existing projects.** Is it because you've hit a challenging obstacle? Are you worried that you'll make a

mistake? Have you been frustrated at the lack of visible results? Are you bored with it?

These are vital questions to ask because sometimes our desire to start something new comes from a fear of confronting a major obstacle. It's okay to eliminate existing goals and projects—just make sure you're doing it for the right reasons.

3. **If you can't replace an old project but you still want to work on the new one, then figure what can be eliminated from your life**. Perhaps you might be willing to reduce your TV time by an hour or two every day, or maybe you can decrease the time spent on your favorite hobby.

    The one thing to keep in mind is that when you add new projects, that extra time has to come from somewhere. So, if you want to add a new focus, you'll need to sacrifice time that's dedicated to something else.

Your life will always be filled with requests for your time. This is especially true as you build your career and your time becomes more sought after. That's when you need to know what's truly important to you and what's not. If you fail to create firm boundaries in your life, then your free time will be chipped away by a constant litany of requests.

Practice #4: Talk to Your Boss about Your Top Projects

While it sounds nice on paper to focus only on projects related to your goals, sometimes you need to face the situation and work on tasks that you might not enjoy.

Obviously, you can't say no to your boss and expect to remain gainfully employed for very long. But if you feel overwhelmed at your job because you have dozens of tasks, you might need to have a candid conversation to relieve some of your job pressures. Here are four strategies for talking to your boss to make sure you're working on the crucial projects that are truly important for the business for which you work:

1. **Do your homework ahead of time.** Identify the two or three regular tasks that provide the biggest impact on the company's bottom line. These should be the activities that you're getting paid to complete. Next, identify the regular tasks that get in the way of these core activities. Ideally, these should be tasks that could be delegated or simply eliminated from your day.

2. **Schedule a time with your boss and briefly mention the reason why you want to meet.** This will give her the opportunity to prepare for the meeting and provide helpful feedback. This advance notice is important because you don't want your boss to feel like you're throwing something at her that requires an immediate decision.

3. **Start the conversation by admitting that you've been struggling to keep up with your work projects.** Talk about the two or three high-leverage tasks that you've identified ahead of

time as being important. Ask your boss if she agrees that these are your priorities. If not, then ask her what she would consider to be important about your job. Keep asking questions and probing until you both can come to an agreement on what you should focus on daily.

4. **Talk about how certain projects and random tasks hinder your ability to focus on these critical tasks**. Usually the biggest culprits are meetings, email, and random disruptions. Sure, they might often seem urgent, but they often can turn into time-sucking tasks that cause you to procrastinate on the activities that are truly important.

   The key to the effectiveness of this step is to not complain about being overworked but to provide solutions on how to fix this issue. These suggestions can include skipping meetings that aren't directly related to your core two or three tasks; eliminating the tasks that don't directly align with your priorities; delegating certain responsibilities that don't align with your core tasks to team members or subordinates; requesting a temporary worker or new employee to lighten the load; and doing certain tasks on a less frequent basis (e.g., weekly instead of daily or monthly instead of weekly).

Sure, going to your boss and admitting that you can't do it all might seem like a scary conversation. But what you're doing is trying to realign your time so you can focus on the activities that generate the biggest profit for the company. If you can show that eliminating the unimportant leads to an increase in productivity, the conversation should be an easy decision when it comes to getting what you want.

Practice #5: Ask Yourself, "What Will My Obituary Say?"

It's easy to say no if you constantly think about the important things in your life. One way to do this is to imagine what will be written in your obituary.

Think of the words in your mind right now. Would you prefer a description that talks about positive things, like how you were a loving parent, great spouse, world traveler, active member of your religious community, and someone who loved life? Or would you choose an obituary that describes how you said yes to every project, worked late at night, and *always* chose your career over your personal goals?

Hopefully, you picked the first option—I know that's the description that I would prefer.

When you align yourself with your goals and consistently say no to anything that doesn't match your current focus, you'll free up time to focus on the activities that are worth reading about when you reach the end of your life.

Those five ways of saying no are firm but don't require burning bridges with the important people in your life. Once you've freed up that extra time, you can create a weekly schedule that focuses on your five core projects, which is what we'll cover in the next step.

Exercise #5: Say No to Anything That Doesn't Match Your Goals

A simple way to avoid procrastination from happening in the first place is to say no when it comes to any task, project, or obligation that doesn't perfectly align with the goals that you've set for yourself.

This will help you in three ways:

1. You remove the feeling of overwhelm that often happens when you've overbooked yourself.

2. You stop agreeing to tasks simply because you don't want disappoint others.

3. You eliminate the likelihood that you'll "tinker" on activities that don't directly relate to your quarterly goals.

You can say no by practicing five habits on a consistent basis:

1. Say no politely but firmly if you know there's no chance you'll follow through on a task. Simply tell the person that you have a few priority projects that require your full attention and you can't afford the distraction.

2. Identify the mandatory tasks that can't be avoided and attach them to an important goal or value.

3. Compare each request for your time to your current five projects. If they don't match, then have the courage to say no to the requester.

4. Talk to your boss about your work projects and make sure that you both agree on the priorities for your job. Then eliminate any task or project that doesn't align with these priorities.

5. Ask yourself, "What will my obituary say?" Make choices based on the values that truly matter.

STEP #5: PLAN YOUR
WEEKLY SCHEDULE

As you've seen so far, one of the philosophies of *How to Stop Procrastinating* is to identify a few core activities in your life, singularly focus on them, and eliminate everything else. Not only does this remove that feeling of overwhelm but it also frees up your time so you're not procrastinating on what's truly important.

So, the question is: "How do I find time to balance all these projects with my day-to-day responsibilities?"

It starts by planning your weekly schedule.

Creating a weekly schedule gives you an opportunity to identify the crucial tasks that you choose to focus on for the next seven days. And it also acts as your first line of defense against those random tasks that could potentially derail your week, causing you to feel overwhelmed.

Now, the weekly review isn't about cramming as many activities as possible into your week. Instead, it's best used to make sure you're maximizing the time spent on your five core projects.

To explain what I mean, let's talk about a popular story that's been passed around productivity and time-management circles. (The original source of the story is unknown.)

Big Rocks and How to Focus on What's Important

The story starts with a philosophy professor who stood up before his class with a large empty jar. He filled the jar to the top with large rocks and asked his students if they thought it was full.

The students said that yes, the jar was indeed full.

He then added small pebbles to the jar, giving the jar a bit of a shake so the pebbles would disperse themselves among the larger rocks.

"Is the jar full now?"

The students agreed that the jar was still full.

The professor then poured sand into the jar to fill up any remaining empty space. The students then agreed that the jar was completely full.

The professor went on to explain that the jar represents everything that's in your life.

The rocks are equivalent to the most important projects and things you have going on, such as spending time with your loved ones and maintaining good health. This means that if the pebbles and the sand were lost, the jar would still be full and your life would still have meaning.

The pebbles represent the things in your life that matter but that you could live without. The pebbles certainly give your life meaning, such as your job, house, and hobbies, but they aren't critical for you to have a meaningful life. These things often come and go and are not permanent or essential to your overall well-being.

Finally, the sand represents the remaining "filler" things in your life and material possessions. These could be small things, such as watching television or running errands. They don't mean much to your life and are likely only done to waste time or get small tasks accomplished.

The metaphor here is that if you start by putting sand into the jar, you will not have room for rocks or pebbles. If you spend all your time on the small and insignificant things, you will run out of room for the things that are actually important.

In order to have a more effective and efficient life, pay attention to the "rocks," because they are critical to your long-term well-being. These should be activities that allow you to improve your career or your health—activities like spending time with your family, exercising, and keeping in touch with relatives that live far away.

While you can always find time to work or do chores, it is important to manage the things that really matter first. The rocks are your priorities, while the other things in your life are represented by pebbles and sand.

The Lesson of the Big Rocks Story

If you want to be effective in your personal and professional life, it's best to have only five rocks in the jar at any given time. These rocks may represent working on a project you want to accomplish, spending time with your family, practicing your faith, focusing on your education, or mentoring other people. Your top five big rocks need to go in the jar first, or they will never get in at all.

If you can identify the important things in your life ahead of time and set aside the time you need to work on them, then in the long run it's okay to procrastinate on the pebbles.

That's why I recommend scheduling your activities with a weekly review and using this schedule as a framework for making those day-to-day decisions about where to focus your efforts.

Once a week (I prefer Fridays or Sundays), look at the next seven days and schedule the activities you'd like to accomplish. You can do this by completing the five following actions.

Action #1: Answer Three Questions

Each weekly review should start with a few minutes of critical thinking about the next seven days. This is the time to mentally review your immediate goals and what *deserves* your attention. You can do this by answering three basic questions:

1. What are my personal obligations?
2. What are my priority projects?
3. How much time do I have?

Your responses to these questions are extremely important, because they will determine the amount of time that can be devoted to your goals during the next seven days.

The lesson here is that you *shouldn't* schedule your week with hundreds of activities, which is the quickest path to that feeling of overwhelm. Instead, it's better to recognize, ahead of time, a realistic amount of time that can be dedicated to your goals and five core projects.

Action #2: Apply the 80/20 Rule to Your Schedule

The 80/20 Rule, originally mentioned by Italian economist Vilfredo Pareto, says that 80% of your results often come from 20% of your efforts. So only a handful of your tasks will produce any sort of measurable result.

This rule can be applied to *any* industry or business. For example, 80% of revenue is generated by 20% of the salespeople; 80% of complaints come from only 20% of customers; and 80% of highway traffic is funneled through 20% of the roads.

My point here is that, no matter what tasks and obligations you need to do weekly, there will *always* be a handful that produce extraordinary results. A few strategies will work well while everything else will be a waste of your time.

You can apply this to procrastination by structuring your schedule in such a way that you focus *only* on just the actions that generate a significant result and proactively ignore almost everything else.

During a weekly review, take a few minutes to carefully consider the answers to these questions:

» What tasks are causing 80% of my problems and unhappiness?

» What core activities have the biggest impact on my career?

» What experiences produce 80% of my fulfillment and happiness?

» Who are the people that cause 80% of my enjoyment and make me feel truly engaged?

» Who are the 20% of people who cause me to feel angry,

unhappy, and unfulfilled?

» What habits make up 80% of my efficiency or effectiveness?

You don't have to ask all these questions every week. But they should always be in the back of your mind when you're creating a weekly schedule. If you get busy, you can simplify everything by asking one simple question: "Does this task help or hinder my ability to work on one of my five goals?"

Be honest with yourself here. Your time is a finite resource. Every minute spent on a time-wasting activity is one less minute that you have for your goals. If you feel something takes away time from those crucial goals, then avoid doing it at *all* costs.

Remember: never let other people's priorities become your own.

Action #3: Block Out Time on a Calendar

This is where the rubber meets the road.

After identifying those 80/20 "big rocks," it's time to put these activities on a calendar.

To get started, I suggest using a calendar where you can schedule your day into 30- to 60-minute increments. You have two options here:

1. Buy a weekly calendar.
2. Use an online calendar, like Google Calendar.

Personally, I prefer the Google Calendar because it syncs with other online tools that I use (like Todoist and Slack). Plus, my wife can look at the schedule on her devices when planning fun activities we can enjoy together. But feel free to pick the tool that works for you.

To get started with blocking out time on your calendar, I recommend five actions:

1. **Begin by blocking out time for the commitments that you already have that involve other people or deadlines.** These are meetings, appointments, and previously scheduled events. There is no flexibility for these commitments, so they should be the first items to put on your calendar.

2. **Block out time for the tasks that are high priorities as well as those that require greater concentration.** These are the rocks and pebbles that have the strongest influence on your life. You can make time for them by looking at your project lists, identifying the actions that need to be completed next, and scheduling time to work on these activities. If you don't make time for these activities, you'll end up focusing on the pebble and sand activities, which don't have as much of a positive impact on your life.

3. **Block out time for personal hobbies, such as reading or going to listen to a speaker talk on a topic that is interesting to you.** You may also find it helpful to block out time to spend with your children doing homework or getting ready for bed. You should also block out time to have a date night with your spouse. It doesn't have to be anything fancy or expensive; just spending the time together to build a healthy relationship will be beneficial to your overall well-being.

4. **Set aside "flexible time" for unexpected tasks and issues that require your immediate attention.** By leaving parts of

your calendar open, you can take care of these issues without derailing your plans to work on the important stuff.

5. **Set aside time to process any ideas that came up during the week**. If you're like me, then you probably have *dozens* of great ideas every week related to your goals. The question is, how do you follow up on them?

   My advice is to process these notes, making one of two choices: (1) take action on it immediately and (2) schedule a time when you'll follow up on it.

Here's how that would work:

If the idea is *actionable*, write out a step-by-step plan for how you'll do it. Simply write down a series of actions you'll take on this idea and then schedule these ideas into your week.

If the idea is *not actionable*, put the idea into an archive folder that's reviewed every month. If you do this for every idea you have, you won't forget to follow up at the right time.

If you want to see an example of what my weekly schedule looks like, then check out the visual walkthrough that I provide in the free companion website.

Action #4: Practice Batching and Create "Theme Days"

If you want to take your time-blocking efforts to the next level, then you can create a weekly schedule where you focus on one type of activity for an extended block of time. This is often called batching tasks.

The benefit of batching is that you remove the stress that often comes from having too many tasks on your to-do list. Instead of trying to tackle everything on one day, you set aside time each week to singularly focus on similar tasks.

For instance, you can batch activities like responding to email, posting on social media, returning phone calls, going to appointments, and handling administrative tasks. These can be done in blocks throughout the day. Any task that you regularly do can be batched with similar tasks.

Now, if you want to take batching one step further, you can create what are known as "theme days." The idea of theme days is to create multiple categories for your career and then block out time each week where you focus on *just* these activities. This focus block can be part of a day or a whole day that's dedicated to one activity. It's the perfect strategy for anyone who needs to wear multiple hats for their job and feels overwhelmed by all that they need to do daily.

For instance, besides my daily habit of writing, there are a few areas of my business that can be grouped together into a single block of time. Here's what this looks like in my typical week:

» Mondays: writing (extra writing in addition to my daily habit).

» Tuesdays: book marketing.

» Wednesdays: conversations and interviews.

» Thursdays: blog optimization.

» Friday: writing and administrative tasks.

» Saturday: family time.

» Sunday: family time.

The beauty of themed days is that they remove much of the stress you regularly experience. When you know that on each day you have to worry about only one thing, it becomes much simpler to ignore all those other obligations that weigh on your mind. Your job is to simply focus on one type of task and work diligently on it.

Action #5: Set Aside Time for Deep Work

If you work in a career field that requires a heightened amount of focus, then you would benefit by blocking off time to focus on what's called Deep Work.

Deep Work is a term that Cal Newport coined in his book appropriately titled *Deep Work*. It refers to professional activities that are done without any distractions while you're in a state of deep concentration. This focus can push your cognitive abilities to their limit.

Without Deep Work, you tend to stay on a superficial level of thought without ever reaching your full potential. The classic example of this is someone who multitasks on tasks like writing a report, checking social media, and texting their friends. Then they wonder why they always feel rushed and never achieve anything of importance.

The key to Deep Work is to guard your time at all costs. While this may seem simple, think about how often you find yourself mindlessly going through work that should be meaningful while breaking your concentration every few minutes to answer your phone or check your email.

There are several things that you must do to be able to accomplish Deep Work. When it comes to social media, either don't be a part of it or leave it for a very specific time of day that is far away from your working hours. Remove the apps from your phone so you're not tempted to check out these sites in the middle of the workday. People who are the most successful don't spend their hours mindlessly scrolling through social media feeds to see what other people are doing. Instead, they focus on themselves and their work.

Additionally, make firm commitments that you cannot back out of. This will give you strict deadlines to adhere to, which will likely help keep you on track. You are much less likely to procrastinate on a task if someone else is depending on you as well.

You also need to be well aware of what tends to distract you the most and address it head on. Is your phone ringing all day, making you change your course of thought several times each hour? Do you work close to people who talk out loud all day long and you can't help but listen to the conversation? Pinpoint what is distracting you so you can eliminate the issue.

People often get distracted by the pebbles or sand in their lives. However, if you proactively set aside adequate time for the important rocks first, then you will know that no matter what happens in life, you have already taken care of the things that truly matter.

Deep Work helps fight procrastination because it requires you to set aside time for the important stuff in your life. Avoiding "time vampires" is key, because while they may seem important at the time, they aren't in the long run.

Exercise #6: Plan Your Weekly Schedule

Creating a weekly schedule gives you an opportunity to identify the crucial tasks that you choose to focus on for the next seven days. It also acts as your first line of defense against those random tasks that could potentially derail your week, causing you to feel overwhelmed.

To get started, set aside a few hours, preferably on Sundays, to schedule the tasks you'd like to accomplish in the next seven days. You should focus on five core actions during this review session:

Action #1: Answer Three Questions

Determine what deserves your attention by answering three basic questions:

1. What are my personal obligations?
2. What are my priority projects?
3. How much time do I have this week?

Action #2: Apply the 80/20 Rule to Your Schedule

Apply the 80/20 Rule to your schedule by spending as much time as possible focusing on the actions that generate a significant result. You can do this by scheduling activities based on the answers to these questions:

» What tasks are causing 80% of my problems and unhappiness?

» What core activities have the biggest impact on my career?

» What experiences produce 80% of my fulfillment and happiness?

» Who are the people that cause 80% of my enjoyment and make me feel truly engaged?

» Who are the 20% of people who cause me to feel angry, unhappy, and unfulfilled?

» What habits make up 80% of my efficiency or effectiveness?

If you get busy, you can simplify everything by answering one question about the tasks you're scheduling: "Does this task help or hinder my ability to work on one of my five goals?"

Action #3: Block Out Time on a Calendar

Block out time on a calendar by scheduling time for your priority tasks, personal hobbies, and "flex time" to reflect on new opportunities or take action on any emergencies that pop up during the week.

Action #4: Practice Batching and Create "Theme Days"

Practice batching by grouping similar tasks together at a specific time or on a theme day.

Action #5: Set Aside Time for Deep Work

Set aside time for Deep Work, where you eliminate all distractions and completely focus on an activity that requires deep concentration.

STEP #6: IMPLEMENT 14 DAILY PRACTICES TO OVERCOME PROCRASTINATION

We've spent much of the book covering topics like identifying your core projects, creating S.M.A.R.T. goals, saying no to low-priority tasks, and planning your weekly schedule. But we haven't talked about how to handle those day-to-day moments when you feel that urge to procrastinate.

The reason I waited until now is because procrastination is often a symptom of a larger issue when it comes to managing your time. I feel when you learn the *right way* to manage your time daily (using what I've discussed in Step #1 through Step #5), you'll eliminate many of the issues that cause procrastination.

That said, I do recognize that your life might be a daily struggle of deciding to focus on the activities you're supposed to be doing while resisting the temptation to skip what you've planned for the day.

So, in this section, I'll cover 14 strategies to help you take action on tasks—even when you don't feel a lack of motivation.

This step has a "choose your own adventure" list of ideas. This means you *don't* need to do all of them to overcome procrastination. Instead,

I encourage you to pick and choose the ones that work well for your personal situation.

Let's get to it.

Practice #1: Resolve Any Potential Emergency

Throughout this book, I've mentioned many strategies for managing your time and increasing your productivity. While I think these things are important, they pale in comparison to the importance of resolving any potential emergency.

Think back to the story about my father that I told at the start of the book. He made a small decision that had a lasting, positive impact on his life. But he could have chosen a different path, which might have led to his death.

My point? If you live an unbalanced life, focusing only on work projects and ignoring everything else, you could be missing a major warning sign of a potential catastrophe.

We all have those moments that require us to immediately drop what we're doing and take care of an unexpected priority. This can include a death in the family, a sick child, or your furnace breaking in the middle of winter.

These scenarios can't wait until your next open block of time. Instead, you often need to cancel everything on your calendar and take care of these issues immediately.

On the other hand, there are scenarios that start out as small things, but could transform into catastrophic events for you or your family.

These can be issues like experiencing chest pain, receiving a letter from the government, getting a phone call from your child's teacher, or hearing from a depressed friend in the middle of the night.

At first, none of these scenarios might seem like an emergency. So, it's easy to let them slip through cracks—especially if you're a busy person. They don't come with a warning sign like the other emergencies in life.

But if you're someone who already procrastinates, then you run the risk of allowing these issues to snowball into a catastrophic event.

As we've discussed, ignoring potential emergencies can lead to death, divorce, suicide, financial ruin, and other horrible situations. No matter how busy you might be, it's always important to immediately address any situation that *could be* an emergency.

This can be done by asking yourself a few questions:

» What is the worst-case scenario if I ignore this issue?

» How would this potential emergency negatively affect my friends and family?

» What are the not-so-important tasks or obligations that I can put off to take care of this potential emergency?

» What simple actions can I take *today* to resolve this issue?

» If it's not a life-threatening issue and I don't have time to address it today, when is the soonest I can deal with it?

In the book *The Top Five Regrets of the Dying*, Bronnie Ware shared her experiences as a palliative care nurse who worked with people in the last few weeks of their lives. Her patients frequently spoke of the things they wished they had done differently. The one regret that sticks out to me is the wish that they hadn't worked so hard during their life.

I feel this is an important lesson, because it's easy to get wrapped up in the daily grind and ignore the issues that don't seem important but can turn into true emergencies if left ignored. Sure, you might not "have time" to take care of the unexpected. But it's also a matter of priorities. No job, task, meeting, or appointment is worth putting something off that could derail your life or the lives of your loved ones.

My suggestion is whenever something comes up, stop what you're doing and take care of it right away.

Have that candid conversation with your spouse.

Make an appointment with a doctor if something doesn't feel right.

Call back your friend who sounds depressed.

Open that scary letter from the government and immediately address it.

Sure, none of these scenarios might be convenient, but I guarantee that taking care of them immediately will prevent scarier issues down the road.

Practice #2: Do a 5- to 10-Minute Daily Review

A simple way to fight procrastination is with a 5- to 10-minute review session. The idea here is to spend a few minutes going over the day's priorities and identifying the tasks that will have the strongest influence on your immediate goals. You should ask yourself these key questions during the review session:

» What appointments and meetings require me to be somewhere at a set time?

» Are there any emergency emails that need to be immediately addressed?

» What specific tasks, which relate to the batches or blocks of time that I've scheduled for the day, can I complete?

» Is there an appointment or activity that could take longer than expected? How will this change my schedule if it does spill over into another task's time?

» What are the 80/20 tasks that will have the biggest impact on my long-term success?

» How does each task relate to my quarterly S.M.A.R.T. goals?

» What is the hardest, most challenging task that I'm dreading?

This quick review session is critical because it provides structure for each day. When you constantly remind yourself which tasks are important, it'll be hard to put them off because you will recognize that your inaction will negatively affect your immediate goals.

Practice #3: Focus On Your MITs

It's easy to feel overwhelmed (and then procrastinate) if you start the day with a to-do list full of tasks, appointments, and projects. You can simplify your list by identifying the tasks that have the biggest impact on your career or life and do them first thing in the morning. This is a concept commonly known as your most important tasks (MITs).

My suggestion is to pick from one to three MITs that absolutely must be completed by the end of the day. Two should relate to an urgent project with an immediate deadline and one should be part of a long-term goal.

For instance, many years ago, I determined that one of my core 80/20 activities is writing. So, even if I have a bunch of urgent tasks that are due at the end of the day, I always set aside at least 30 minutes for this task—usually right after my morning routine. From there, I spend the rest of my morning on the other two MITs. By focusing on important activities right away, I create an energized state that allows me to work on any project in the afternoon.

Practice #4: Eat the Frog

In his classic book on how to overcome procrastination, *Eat That Frog!*, Brian Tracy suggests that the best way to begin your day is to, well, "eat that frog." The idea stems from a Mark Twain quote:

> If the first thing you do each morning is to eat a live frog, you can go through the day with the satisfaction of knowing that that is probably the worst thing that is going to happen to you all day long.

Tracy's point is if you can complete the hardest task first, then you'll begin with a major win that will make all the successive tasks or chores seem less daunting. It also will be motivating knowing that you've already tackled the one thing that you are most likely to procrastinate on.

This advice is perfect for anyone who frequently puts off tasks that require focus and hard work. If you can commit yourself to just getting started and working on your hardest task right away, then you'll discover that's it probably not as bad as you thought.

Once again, let's go back to my writing example. This is a task that I'll frequently dread or not want to do. But I also know that if I put it off for later in the day, then I'll increase the likelihood that I'll skip it or get distracted by another activity.

By committing myself to eat the frog first thing in the morning, I know that after 30–60 minutes of effort, I've already completed the most challenging task for the day.

Trust me: one of the most motivating experiences is knowing you've already completed the hardest task before 9:00 a.m.

Practice #5: Use the Eisenhower Matrix to Make Quick Decisions

While it's great to imagine a perfect workday where you're able to work on just your MITs in isolation, this rarely happens in the real world. If you're like most people, your day is filled with a steady stream of small emergencies, random disruptions, and unexpected changes. These can feel overwhelming if you don't have a framework that allows you to separate the important from the not-so-important.

That's why I recommend using a simple decision-making strategy called the Eisenhower Matrix, so named because Dwight Eisenhower, prior to becoming the 34th president of the United States, served as a general in the army and as the Allied forces' supreme commander during World War II.

During his time in the army, Eisenhower was faced with many tough decisions concerning the tasks he had to focus on every day. This led him to invent a principle that helps us today by prioritizing our tasks by urgency and importance. If this strategy was good enough to help Eisenhower lead hundreds of thousands of people, then it's probably good enough to help with your procrastination issue. (Stephen Covey, author of *The 7 Habits of Highly Effective People*, further popularized Eisenhower's concept by supporting Eisenhower's use of four quadrants to determine the urgency of one's tasks.)

The Eisenhower Matrix prioritizes your tasks by urgency and importance, which results in four quadrants that each require a separate approach and strategy. In addition to sorting tasks by urgency and importance, the matrix also identifies tasks that you should either delegate or completely remove from your life. Following is a brief overview of this system. (If you want a downloadable version of this matrix, then you can grab a copy by signing up for the free companion website.)

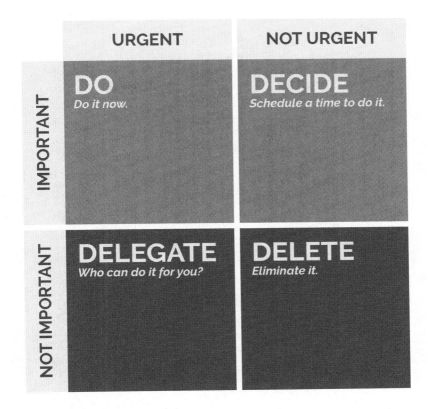

Quadrant 1 (Q1): Urgent and Important

Quadrant 1 (Q1) tasks are the "do first" tasks, because they are critical for your life or career in some way and need to be finished right away. They are the tasks that need to be done in order to avoid negative consequences. It's important to be able to manage the tasks that are in Q1 before anything else, so you want to get these tasks done as soon as possible.

An example of a Q1 task in your career may be answering a time-sensitive email from a client or finishing a report that's due by the end of the day.

This matrix can also be used in your personal life. Examples of Q1 tasks in your personal life may be a crying baby, a medical emergency, or something burning in the oven.

Quadrant 2 (Q2): Important but not Urgent

Quadrant 2 (Q2) are the "decide when" tasks, because while they can have an amazing impact on your life, they don't seem immediately critical like the Q1 tasks that need to be done right away.

Simply put, Q2 tasks usually relate to your long-term goals. In an ideal world, this is where you want to invest most of your time. But unfortunately, this is the area that's the easiest to ignore because you're too focused on the priorities from the other quadrants.

What are some examples of these tasks? Well, exercising is important to your health. So is spending time with your family or working on a certificate that will improve your career path. Usually, nobody is pushing you to complete Q2 activities, so it's easy to let these tasks fall by the wayside.

Quadrant 3 (Q3): Urgent but not Important

Quadrant 3 (Q3) tasks are the "delegate it" tasks, because while they seem urgent, they can often be automated or passed off to someone who is better qualified to handle them.

This is the quadrant for those tasks that, in hindsight, turned out to be not very important. Taking on Q3 tasks often occurs when someone asks you to do something that does not directly benefit you or get you closer to achieving your goals. For Q3 tasks, it's important to learn and remember how to delegate certain things.

When you think something is urgent when it isn't, it's usually caused by an outside source of distraction—like checking your email or phone or responding to people as soon as they try to contact you. You may think it is urgent at the moment, so you stop what you're doing to tend to the matter, but in retrospect, the task wasn't that crucial.

If you're in the middle of working on a project and the phone rings, it's not important for you to answer it. So, you can delegate this task to someone else. It may seem urgent while it is ringing, but a task like this can usually be handled by other people. (Don't worry, we'll talk about *how* later in the book.)

Quadrant 4 (Q4): Not Important and not Urgent

Quadrant 4 (Q4) tasks are the "delete it" tasks, because they are the activities you should avoid at all costs. They are simply a complete waste of your time. If you are able to identify and eliminate all of your Q4 tasks, then you can free up much-needed time that can be reinvested in Q2 tasks.

Some examples of Q4 tasks are playing video games, watching television shows, mindlessly browsing the web, or fulfilling obligations that are other people's priorities.

Does that mean nothing in Q4 should be a part of your life?

The short answer is no.

Having a balance between your professional and personal life is important, and downtime helps you regain your energy. The challenge here is to spend most of your time in Q2 and just enough time in Q4 to relax.

How to Use the Eisenhower Matrix to Overcome Procrastination

To get started with the Eisenhower Matrix, I recommend a simple exercise:

» Print out the list that's included in the companion website or create one on your own that's divided into the four sections previously described.

» Make seven copies of a blank grid for each week.

» Each day, write down the tasks that you'd like to accomplish, putting them in the appropriate quadrant.

» Whenever something new pops up, take a minute or two to think about the nature of the task and put it in the appropriate quadrant.

» At the end of the week, when all of the grids are full, evaluate how effectively you spent your time and whether your process needs to be reorganized. Keep adjusting your schedule until you're spending as much time as possible completing Q1 and Q2 activities.

Don't worry if at first you find that most of your time is spent in "reaction mode," with you mostly focusing on urgent activities in Q1 and Q3.

It's normal to get fixated on the stuff that has a definitive deadline. But if you keep tracking your tasks using this matrix, asking yourself why you do each activity, and then redesigning your schedule, you'll discover it's not that hard to structure each day on the tasks that have the biggest impact on your long-term success.

Practice #6: Complete Quick Tasks Immediately

Have you ever procrastinated on a task that doesn't require much effort, like cleaning the dishes after a meal, making a phone call, looking up a phone number, or sending an email? You know it doesn't take much effort to complete. Yet you keep putting it off because you're too busy or you think you don't have time to do it.

This often happens because we fail to complete those small, seemingly unimportant tasks. By ignoring the activities that can be easily resolved, we build them up in our mind as being tougher than they actually are. On the other hand, if you learn to take immediate actions on small tasks, then you'll prevent them from piling up. There are two strategies that can help you do this.

First, there is the Two-Minute Rule that David Allen recommends in *Getting Things Done*. If you know a task takes only a few minutes, then do it right away instead of writing it down on your to-do list or swearing that you'll do it later.

Whenever you think of something that needs done, ask yourself: "How long will this take?"

If it's only a minute or two, then do it right away instead of putting it off. You'll find that doing this consistently will remove much of the negativity that happens when you have a lengthy list of tasks to complete.

On the other hand, if a task requires more than a few minutes of effort, then put it on your calendar and schedule time when you can take care of it.

The second strategy, closely related to the Two-Minute Rule, is to "single-handle" *every task*. Think of all the times you've opened an email, realized it required an action that you don't have time to complete, so you put it off until later. Then when "later" comes, you open the same message, read it again, and then remember that the email requires a follow-up action.

Single-handling can remove the stress created by the small tasks you procrastinate on because it forces you to *complete* any task that you start. The idea here is whenever you begin something, you need to see it to its conclusion.

Here are a few examples:

» Responding to an email when you open it or scheduling the specific action that needed to "process" the message.

» Rinsing a dish and putting it in the dishwasher after a meal instead of putting it in the sink.

» Discarding junk mail into a recycling bin right when you receive it.

» Putting away your clothes after wearing them instead of tossing them on a chair.

» Returning phone calls immediately whenever you receive a voice mail.

It's easy to procrastinate when you feel overwhelmed by your daily tasks, but if you take an extra minute or two to complete a simple action, you'll find that it's easy to eliminate some of the stress that comes from having a huge list of small tasks.

Practice #7: Create a Mini Habit for Challenging Tasks

As we've discussed, one reason people procrastinate is they know a task will require hard work. You'll need to mentally (or physically) push yourself, so you keep putting it off and doing something else that results in a dopamine rush of instant gratification. It's perfectly normal to avoid doing something you know might be unpleasant. But if you're often struggling to get started on a challenging task, then a quick fix for that is to use the mini-habits strategy.

"Mini habits" is a term coined by my friend Stephen Guise, which appears in the book of the same name. The purpose of mini habits is to remove the resistance that you feel when it comes to starting a difficult (or time-consuming) task. It's easy to schedule an activity into your day (like running for an hour), but it's hard to complete when you feel a lack of interest.

Mini habits work because they eliminate motivation from the equation. Instead of setting an extremely challenging goal, you set a "lowball" goal that makes it super simple to get started. Let's go over a scenario in the following paragraphs that illustrate this point.

Imagine you set a goal to exercise for 30 minutes. Everything goes perfectly the first week. You join a gym, attend a few classes, and enjoy the endorphin rush of frequent exercise.

One day, your boss asks you to work late, so you're forced to skip your scheduled class. You tell yourself, "That's okay, I'll do it tomorrow." But in the back of your mind, you start to doubt your commitment to this new exercise habit.

This pattern repeats itself over the next few weeks. You miss classes for a variety of reasons: Your kid has the flu. You didn't pack your gym clothes. The roads are covered in snow. You have to wash your cat. Suddenly, this "30 minutes of exercise time" has turned into a task that feels impossible to do consistently. Stinks, doesn't it?

The mini-habit concept prevents this scenario, because it eliminates that overwhelmed feeling you get when you think a task is too difficult to complete. To quote Stephen:

> When people try to change, they usually try to get amped up for the change, but no matter how badly you want the change, you haven't changed yet! As motivation wanes, so does progress. *You don't need more motivation, you need a strategy that can leverage the abilities of the current you into a better you.*

In other words, the simplest, most effective way to create a lasting change is to create a goal that might seem too easy to complete but is also so easy that you can do it on a consistent basis.

So, if you're finding yourself frequently procrastinating on a specific activity, then create the simplest possible habit you can think of to force yourself to get started. Here are a few examples:

» *Want to start writing?* Set a goal to write one sentence.

» *Want to run more?* Set a goal to put on your exercise clothes.

» *Want to improve your sales record?* Set a goal to pick up the phone and call the first lead.

» *Want to improve your grades?* Set a goal to spend five minutes reviewing your notes.

» *Want to improve your nutrition?* Set a goal to eat one mouthful of a salad.

I'll admit these goals seem ridiculously simple. But that's the point—each activity is completely doable, no matter what your schedule is like. If you can push yourself to just get started, then often you'll find yourself doing more of an activity than you initially anticipated.

Practice #8: Build Elephant Habits for Ongoing Projects

We've all heard this piece of advice before: "How do you eat an elephant? One bite at a time."

The idea is that whenever you're faced with a large, complex goal, all you need to do is chip away at it in small chunks.

Unfortunately, many people don't apply this mindset to their lives. When they're forced to tackle large projects, they procrastinate or even avoid them completely because the tasks seem insurmountable.

You, on the other hand, can take any large project and chip away at it using what I call elephant habits, which I discussed at length in my book *Habit Stacking: 127 Small Changes to Improve Your Health, Wealth, and Happiness.*

Elephant habits are designed to overcome the natural resistance we all feel whenever we're forced to do a potentially unpleasant, massive project. We know it must be done, but we avoid starting because dedicating a few days to it sounds as fun as getting a root canal. Thankfully, an elephant habit will help you complete a project one bite at a time.

The goal here is to chip away at a simple but time-consuming project in 5- to 15-minute daily increments. You can do this with many of the larger tasks on your to-do list, such as:

» decluttering your home;

» packing for a move;

» organizing your paperwork (e.g., in preparation for tax season);

» studying for an exam;

» completing a time-consuming homework assignment; or

» reading a difficult book.

I use elephant habits whenever I'm faced with something unpleasant. Rather than building it up in my mind as a horrific ordeal, I overcome inertia by scheduling a 15-minute daily block where I can chip away at the project. (Usually, it's tacked on to my morning routine or part of an existing habit stack, which we'll cover in the next step.)

Elephant habits have a similar framework to the mini-habits concept that we've just discussed. When you tell yourself that a task takes "only" five minutes of your time, it's easier to convince yourself to get started. And usually, once you get started, you'll find yourself doing more of that activity than you originally planned.

Practice #9: Use Sprints to Work On Challenging Projects

Smart workers overcome their procrastination tendencies by condensing their efforts into short "sprints" and tracking them with a timer. The idea here is to work for a short period of time and then give yourself frequent breaks. The benefit of these sprints is that it's easy to push yourself to get started when you know there is a clear stopping and starting point. Once you complete a sprint, you can take a quick break and then start a second sprint.

The strategy that I recommend for completing these sprints is a system called the Pomodoro Technique. The Pomodoro Technique is a popular time-blocking system, created in the 1980s by Francesco Cirillo, that has been embraced by entrepreneurs and work-efficiency experts.

Cirillo recognized that humans can focus for only a limited amount of time before becoming distracted. He found that it's better to create a system where people focus for a condensed period and then proactively take a break before beginning the next sprint.

He named his technique after a popular kitchen timer that looks like a tomato (hence the name *pomodoro*, which is Italian for *tomato*). The timer was used like any old kitchen timer, but Cirillo experimented with time blocking until he discovered the most effective usage of time blocks (for efficiency in work production).

When using the Pomodoro Technique, you:

» choose a task (e.g., writing);

» set a timer for 25 minutes;

» work for 25 minutes without succumbing to *any* distractions;

» take a 5-minute break by getting up and walking around;

» go back to work for another 25 minutes; and

» after every four time-blocks, take a 15- to 30-minute break.

You might assume that this technique is not as effective as working without breaks. But think back to those times when you tried to do a task for an extended period of time. In all likelihood, you were energized at first, then you reached a point when your concentration dropped off. Finally, you probably felt the urge to do anything *besides* your current task.

The Pomodoro Technique prevents these distractions because it keeps your mind fresh and focused. With the scheduled breaks, you have an opportunity to take a few minutes off to relax. Even though you're working for less time, the quality of the content will be better than what's normally created at the tail end of a marathon session.

If you're interested in the Pomodoro Technique, you might want to download one of the following programs:

» Team Viz (a program that syncs between your computer and mobile phone)

» Pomodoro Time Management by Rapid Rabbit (iPhone and iPad apps)

» Pomodoro Timer (PC users)

» Pomodoro (Mac users)

» Pomodoro (Android users)

When it comes to time blocking, the amount of time you choose really depends on your personal preference. I like the Pomodoro Technique because it has a nice symmetry. The 25 minutes on and 5 minutes off adds up to 30 minutes. You can schedule these 30-minute blocks throughout the day and use these sprints to complete those challenging tasks that you would normally procrastinate on.

Practice #10: Build the Discomfort Habit

One of the best strategies you can use to permanently overcome procrastination is to *become comfortable being uncomfortable*. Mastering this skill can allow you to do pretty much anything. You can stop procrastinating, begin that exercise regimen, eat healthier, get that degree, speak in public, and overcome specific challenges in your life.

Truthfully, most people choose to avoid being uncomfortable. Just the thought of working hard or experiencing some level of pain is the main reason they fail to change their habits.

For example, many people choose to live a sedentary life because exercising takes too much effort. It is easier to simply sit at a desk or lie on the couch all day. Now, exercise isn't torture; it's just something that takes some effort and a willingness to experience discomfort.

Similarly, when people try to push aside their junk food and start eating a healthy diet, they often discover that the new food on their plate is bland, unexciting, and not filling. Changing what your taste buds are used to is a bit uncomfortable, but to be honest, you can retrain your taste buds if you are willing to push through a little discomfort.

Discomfort is not a bad thing—it's just doing something that's not part of your normal routine. As people avoid discomfort, they pay the price of not being able to change things in their lives, not living a healthy life, and not being open to new adventures.

The important thing to remember here is that a little discomfort is healthy. It can actually turn something you perceive as dreadful into an enjoyable habit—if you're willing to push yourself at first. So, let's talk about how to do that.

How to Master Discomfort

If you choose to master discomfort, you can do it comfortably. While this may sound counterintuitive, it means that you do things at your own pace and a little bit at a time. If you're nervous about being uncomfortable and try to beat your nerves with an overly grueling activity, there is a good chance that you will give up and return to what you are familiar with.

Here are five steps to success (as outlined by Leo Babauta in an article titled "Discomfort Zone: How to Master the Universe"):

1. Choose an easy task. Start with something small. If your goal is to increase your activity level, start with walking outside for 30 minutes a day. You already know how to walk, so this won't add any complications to something that you already do every day. Do not worry about your pace or how far you are able to go—just walk.

2. Just do a little. If you don't want to start with 30 minutes of something that you are not used to doing, start with 5 minutes. It doesn't matter where you choose to start, just make sure that you do.

3. Gradually push yourself out of your comfort zone. When you want to stop, push yourself just a bit further. Begin to sit through the moments of discomfort so you can get used to the feeling and see how it comes and goes. Each time you go back and try to do something, push through one more phase

of discomfort to help you gradually learn how to comfortably leave your comfort zone.

4. Pay attention to your discomfort. Pay attention to your thoughts as you become uncomfortable. Do you start to have negative thoughts or complain silently in your head? Do you start looking for a way out? How do your thoughts change if you stick with the discomfort and push your way through?

5. Smile. Learning how to smile while being uncomfortable can help you be happy with discomfort. Smiling sends a message to your brain that you are happy and everything is fine. It also sends the message to other people that you are confident in what you are doing, which will likely make you feel more comfortable as well.

Once you become comfortable with being uncomfortable, you'll build the mental willpower to get started on a task—even when you initially feel like procrastinating.

Practicing discomfort is like building a muscle. If you work at accepting discomfort regularly, you'll realize that getting started with any task isn't as bad as you think. Even if you're dreading beginning a task, challenge yourself to do it for just five minutes. You'll probably discover that it's not as bad as you anticipated it would be.

Practice #11: Remove Hidden Blocks with the Awareness Habit

A golden nugget that I learned from Leo Babauta's article "Building Awareness of the Procrastination Urge" is that one of the simplest ways to beat procrastination is to build what he calls the awareness habit.

The major challenge that folks have with procrastination is they're often unaware that they're even doing it. That's why a simple way to prevent it is to create a habit where you track your impulses to procrastinate.

Here are a few techniques that Babauta recommends:

» **Create reminders**. Write notes to yourself on pieces of paper, and put them around the areas you usually procrastinate. You could even create a wallpaper message on your computer or phone, using a phrase like "Be aware!" to act as a reminder to not procrastinate on what's important.

» **Use tally marks**. Carry around a small notepad and a pen. Throughout the day, when you notice yourself getting the urge to procrastinate, simply put a little tally mark on the paper. These tally marks are not necessarily a good or bad thing. Instead, they act as a way for you to build awareness of your desire to procrastinate.

» **Log it daily**. Finally, at the end of the day, you should track the awareness habit as something that you successfully completed. Like any other habit, you should track the fact that you did it throughout the day. You can even sign up on Coach.me to track the awareness habit.

Once you've developed the habit of asking questions about your procrastination, you can use this information to immediately address any limiting belief that you might have.

To get started, ask yourself questions like:

> » What reason do I have for putting off this task?
>
> » Why do I feel it's so tough to do?
>
> » How many times have I successfully done it in the past?
>
> » What did I do then to get started?
>
> » What is the easiest step that I can do right now to get started?

Recognizing that you procrastinate on specific tasks is the best way to break this habit. When you develop the awareness habit, you'll start to recognize the specific patterns and triggers that cause you to skip an activity. Then all you need to do is to create a plan for how you'll respond whenever you feel the temptation to procrastinate.

Practice #12: Bundle Rewards with Actions

In a blog article titled "How to Stop Procrastinating and Boost Your Willpower by Using 'Temptation Bundling,'" James Clear talks about a concept called temptation bundling, which comes from the work of Katy Milkman. The idea here is simple: you create a rule where you're allowed to engage in a specific enjoyable experience only while you're engaging in an activity that has a positive long-term impact on your life.

In his article, Clear describes examples of temptation bundling:

» "Only listen to audiobooks or podcasts you love while exercising."

» "Only get a pedicure while processing overdue work emails."

» "Only watch your favorite show while ironing or doing household chores."

» "Only eat at your favorite restaurant when conducting your monthly meeting with a difficult colleague."

It's simple to implement the temptation bundling strategy. Just create a list with two columns:

1. In the first column, write down all the activities that you enjoy and find pleasure in.

2. In the second column, put down the tasks that you frequently procrastinate on.

You'll find the temptation bundling is perfect for those important but not urgent Q2 tasks. These are the activities that you know you're *supposed* to do but that you keep putting off because they don't seem as urgent your day-to-day activities.

By attaching small rewards to the habits related to your long-term goals, you'll be adding a little bit of enjoyment to the activities that often feel grueling.

Practice #13: Attach All Tasks to a Goal

It's amazing how a shift in perspective can be enough to motivate you. Whenever you have a task that you've been dreading, ask yourself: "How does this relate to one of my important goals?"

Odds are you'll realize that even the most mundane activity is related to a value you hold dear.

As an example, while I'm responsible for doing the dishes in my house, it's not an activity that I find pleasurable. At no point in the day do I say to myself: "Ooohhh, I can't wait to get to those dishes."

That said, I do them happily, because this task is part of the large, *really* important value of building a great relationship with my wife. She likes to live in a clean, organized household. And I like to make her happy. This means that doing the dishes has become one part of the important goal of maintaining a quality marriage.

You can apply this mindset to any task that you've been avoiding. Simply make a list of your personal and professional responsibilities. Then connect each one to an important value or goal. And whenever you're not in the mood to get started, remind yourself of how it relates to one of your long-term goals.

Practice #14: Create Accountability for Your Tasks

You've probably heard about the law of inertia (also known as Newton's first law of motion). If you haven't, the law states that "an object at rest stays at rest and an object in motion stays in motion with the same speed and in the same direction unless acted upon by an unbalanced force."

In other words, if your natural tendency is to lounge around before starting the day, then you'll need an extra "push" to force you into action. People often procrastinate because it's easier to do nothing than it is to push themselves to do a potentially unpleasant task.

That's why one of the biggest lessons I've learned about habit development is to add *accountability* for every major goal.

It's not enough to make a personal commitment. The big things in life require a solid action plan and a support network to tap into whenever you encounter an obstacle. This is true for your career trajectory *and* your personal development. When you have someone to cheer on your successes (or kick you in the butt when you're slacking), you're less likely to give up.

There are a variety of ways to be accountable, like posting your progress on social media accounts or telling the people in your life about your new routine, but I have found that there are three strategies that get the best results.

The first is to use Beeminder, which is a habit-building app on steroids. Instead of relying on self-reporting to track your habits, Beeminder syncs with a variety of apps (like Gmail, Fitbit, and RescueTime) to make sure you follow through with your commitments. If you fail to achieve a target goal, then Beeminder will charge you money. Sounds hard-core, right?

In my opinion, the best use of Beeminder is to use the location app on your cell phone when you're at the gym and then create a "commitment contract" with Beeminder where you promise to go to this location for a specific amount of time each week. If you don't follow through, you'll have to pay money to Beeminder.

The second option is to use Coach.me, which is another great app for maintaining and sticking to new habits. It's like having a coach in your pocket, for better and for worse. You'll be held accountable for your task by adding it as a habit and checking in every single day when it's been completed. Trust me—the simple act of knowing that you have to update people on your progress is motivation enough to stick to a habit-stacking routine.

Finally, you can work with an accountability partner with whom you share your breakthroughs, challenges, and future plans. This is a great way to get a kick in the butt whenever you feel a wane in motivation. It's also valuable to have someone you can confide in whenever you have a challenge that requires a second opinion.

If you're interested in finding prospective accountability partners, be sure to check out my Facebook group, HabitsGroup.com, which has over 2,000 members. Every month, we create a thread where members can connect with one another and become accountability partners.

Exercise #7: Implement 14 Daily Practices to Overcome Procrastination

Overcoming procrastination is a daily struggle that often requires you to take action—even when a specific activity is the last thing that you feel like working on. That's why I recommend using 14 practices that will help you avoid procrastinating on the tasks you have scheduled for the day.

Practice #1: Resolve Any Potential Emergency

Resolve all potential emergencies by answering (and taking action on) a series of questions:

» What is the worst-case scenario if I ignore this issue?

» How would this potential emergency negatively affect my friends and family?

» What are the not-so-important tasks or obligations that I can put off to take care of this potential emergency?

» What simple actions can I take *today* to resolve this issue?

» If it's not a life-threatening issue and I don't have time to address it today, when is the soonest I can take care of it?

Practice #2: Do a 5- to 10-Minute Daily Review

Do a 5- to 10-minute daily review to make sure you're focusing on the right things every day:

» What appointments and meetings require me to be somewhere at a set time?

» Are there any emergency emails that need to be immediately addressed?

» What specific tasks, which relate to the batches or blocks of time that I've scheduled for the day, can I complete?

» Is there an appointment or activity that could take longer than expected? How will this change my schedule if it does spill over into another task's time?

» What are the 80/20 tasks that will have the biggest impact on my long-term success?

» How does each task relate to my quarterly S.M.A.R.T. goals?

» What is the hardest, most challenging task that I'm dreading?

Practice #3: Focus On Your MITs

Start your day by completing 2–3 of your MITs. These are the activities that will have the biggest long-term impact on your career and personal life.

Practice #4: Eat the Frog

Eat the frog by completing the hardest task first, preferably the one task that you know you're most likely to procrastinate on.

Practice #5: Use the Eisenhower Matrix to Make Quick Decisions

Use the Eisenhower Matrix to make quick decisions about every new activity that you *could* work on.

Practice #6: Complete Small Tasks—ASAP

Take action on small tasks by applying the Two-Minute Rule and single-handling most of your daily tasks.

Practice #7: Create a Mini Habit for Challenging Tasks

Create a mini habit for challenging tasks by setting a "lowball" goal that makes it super simple to get started.

Practice #8: Build Elephant Habits for Ongoing Projects

"Eat your elephant" by chipping away at daunting tasks in 5- to 10-minute increments every day.

Practice #9: Use Sprints to Work On Challenging Projects

Use the Pomodoro Technique to work in a series of sprints for large, ongoing projects. You will:

» choose a task (e.g., writing);

» set a timer for 25 minutes;

» work for 25 minutes without succumbing to *any* distractions;

» take a 5-minute break by getting up and walking around;

» go back to work for another 25 minutes; and

» after every four time blocks, take a 15- to 30-minute break.

Practice #10: Build the Discomfort Habit

Build the discomfort habit by becoming comfortable being uncomfortable. This will increase your personal tolerance for completing challenging tasks.

Practice #11: Remove Hidden Blocks with the Awareness Habit

Use the awareness habit to identify the signs indicating you're likely to procrastinate.

Ask yourself questions like these:

» What reason do I have for putting off this task?

» Why do I feel it's so tough to do?

» How many times have I successfully done it in the past?

» What did I do then to get started?

» What is the easiest step that I can do right now to get started?

Practice #12: Bundle Rewards with Actions

Bundle rewards with actions to create a rule where you're allowed to engage in a specific enjoyable experience only when you do something that benefits you in the long term.

Practice #13: Attach All Tasks to a Goal

Attach all tasks to a goal by making a list of your personal and professional responsibilities and connecting each one to an important value or goal.

Practice #14: Create Accountability for Your Tasks

Use accountability to make sure you follow through on your tasks and avoid procrastination. There are three strategies that can help you do this.

First, use Beeminder to charge you money if you fail to complete a specific activity. Next, join Coach.me and use this app to check in whenever you complete a habit related to one of your important goals. Finally, work with an accountability partner with whom you share your breakthroughs, challenges, and future plans.

STEP #7: CREATE YOUR GAME PLAN FOR OVERCOMING PROCRASTINATION

W e've covered a wealth of material in the previous six steps. Sometimes, the advice in these pages requires you to complete one-time, simple actions. Other times, I recommend building habits that help you fight procrastination on an ongoing basis. And occasionally, I've asked you to make the proactive decision to eliminate what's *not working* in your life.

Put simply: *How to Stop Procrastinating* requires a bit of hard work on your part.

The challenge is knowing how to get started.

So, in this final step, I'll wrap up all you've learned with a step-by-step plan that you can use to forever eliminate your procrastination tendencies.

This step is broken down into four core activities that need to be completed:

1. The one-time actions that will set up the framework of identifying what's important in your life and what's not.

2. How to schedule a weekly review session that helps you laser-focus on what needs to be accomplished in the next seven days.

3. A 13-step action plan of how to fight procrastination daily using my habit-stacking concept.

4. Practices you can use to fight procrastination whenever you feel the urge to put off an important task.

Yes, most of the concepts discussed in this step have been covered in previous sections, but what you'll get in the following steps is a simplified version of how to turn the information you've learned into a solid action plan.

Activity #1: Complete Four One-Time Exercises

An effective way to break the cycle of procrastination is to clearly understand your immediate priorities. As we've discussed, one of the primary reasons people procrastinate is they often feel overwhelmed by an avalanche of personal and professional responsibilities.

You can fight that feeling of overwhelm by completing four one-time exercises:

Exercise	Time Required
1. Write down your current commitments and any activities you'd like to do in the next year. Put this list in an app like Evernote or a journal that's always nearby.	30–60 minutes
2. Identify your core values and goals that are important to you. These should relate to activities that make you happy, the experiences where you feel the most alive, and the people that enrich your life. Use value words that act as a reminder of why they are important.	30–60 minutes

Exercise	Time Required
3. Identify your five core projects by jotting down 25 projects or activities that you could focus on in the next year. Then narrow down this list until you pick just five projects. Commit to these five activities for the next quarter and say no to anything else that conflicts with these goals.	30–60 minutes
4. Set a S.M.A.R.T. goal for every three months for each of the five core projects. Each goal should have a specific outcome and a deadline of when you will achieve it. Use these goals as a guideline whenever you feel stuck or if you're wondering how a task fits into your quarterly plan.	30 minutes

Activity #2: Schedule a Weekly Planning Session

Your weekly schedule will become your greatest defense against procrastination and that feeling of overwhelm caused by daily tasks. Not only does the weekly review give you a bird's-eye view of all the tasks that need to be completed but it also provides a realistic look at how much time you actually have every seven days.

To implement this activity, you need to schedule a 60-minute session every week (preferably on a Friday or Sunday). During this block of time, you'll complete five actions:

Action #1: Answer Three Questions

Determine what deserves your attention by answering three basic questions:

1. What are my personal obligations?
2. What are my priority projects?
3. How much time do I have this week?

Action #2: Apply the 80/20 Rule to Your Schedule

Apply the 80/20 Rule by scheduling as much time as possible for the actions that have the biggest impact on your professional and personal life. Be sure to schedule these before anything else.

Action #3: Block Out Time on a Calendar

Block out time on a calendar by scheduling time for your priority tasks, personal hobbies, and flex time to reflect on new opportunities (or emergencies) that pop up during the week.

Action #4: Practice Batching and Create "Theme Days"

Practice batching by grouping similar tasks together at a specific time or on a theme day in which you accomplish a batch of tasks.

Action #5: Set Aside Time for Deep Work

Set aside time for Deep Work, in which you eliminate all distractions and completely focus on an activity that requires deep concentration.

Activity #3: Build an Anti-Procrastination Habit-Stacking Routine

Procrastination can be a daily struggle. Even if you have the perfect schedule full of activities that you know you're supposed to do, sometimes it's hard to force yourself to take that first step on a challenging task. That's why I recommend building a series of actions into your day using my concept of habit stacking, which I cover in my book of the same name.

The habit-stacking concept is built on the premise that it's hard to add multiple new habits to your daily routine. So, instead of trying to remember them all, I recommend *grouping small habits together into a routine and then completing this routine at a specific time each day. You can do all this with a simple 13-step process.* (For detailed instructions on each step, I recommend checking out an overview of habit stacking in the article "13 Steps to Building a Habit Stacking Routine," which appears on my blog.) *For our purposes in this book, however, I describe the 13 steps in an abbreviated form:*

1. Identify an area of your life you'd like to improve, and start with a 5-minute block of habits. This will help you create consistency by making sure that you're sticking with this new routine. Since this is a book about overcoming procrastination, I recommend picking a few of the practices that I mentioned in the previous section.

2. Focus on small wins by picking simple habits that don't require much willpower, like taking a vitamin, weighing yourself, or reviewing your goals. To simplify things, I recommend completing these habits daily:

- Start your day with a quick 5- to 10-minute review session during which you go over your tasks and appointments.

- Identify 2–3 of your most important tasks and commit to completing these before anything else.

- Get started on your hardest task first, preferably the one task that you know you're mostly likely to procrastinate on.

- Say no when it comes to any task, project, or obligation that doesn't perfectly align with the goals that you've set for yourself.

- Create a mini habit for challenging tasks by setting a "lowball" goal that makes it super simple to get started.

- Build elephant habits for ongoing projects by chipping away at them in 5- to 10-minute increments every day.

- Use the Pomodoro Technique to work in a series of sprints for large, challenging projects.

- Take action on small tasks by applying the Two-Minute Rule and single-handling most of your daily tasks.

3. Pick a time, location, or combination of both for when you'll complete the How to Stop Procrastinating stack. Ideally, I recommend completing this routine to start the day because it will set the tone for what you accomplish and how you address those random emergencies.

4. Anchor your stack to a trigger, which is an existing habit you automatically do *every* day, like showering, brushing your teeth, checking your phone, going to the refrigerator, or sitting down

at your desk. This is important because you need to be 100% certain that you won't miss this trigger.

5. Create a logical checklist, which should include the sequence of the actions, how long it takes to complete each item, and where you'll do them.

6. Be accountable by using an app like Coach.me to track your progress and frequently talking to an accountability partner with whom you share your breakthroughs, challenges, and future plans.

7. Create small, enjoyable rewards that help you stick with this routine and hit important milestones. These rewards can include watching your favorite TV show, eating a healthy snack, or relaxing for a few minutes.

8. Focus on repetition by never missing a day. In fact, it's crucial that you stick to the routine—even if you need to skip one or two habits. Consistency is more important than anything else.

9. Avoid breaking the chain by eliminating any excuse for missing a day. Create a doable daily goal that can be achieved no matter what happens, and don't let yourself be talked out of it. Perhaps you'll set a small goal requiring you to only complete two or three habits. The important thing is to set a goal that can be achieved even when you have an off day.

10. Expect the occasional challenge or setback. In fact, it's better if you assume they will happen and then make a plan for how you'll handle them. If you get stuck, review the six challenges that we just covered and implement the advice for your unique obstacle.

11. Schedule the frequency of a stack by committing to this routine as a daily, weekly, or monthly series of actions. My suggestion is to get started with a simple daily routine, but when you want to build more habits, add a weekly or monthly task.

12. Scale-up your stack by adding more habits and increasing the total time of the routine. But be very cautious with this step. If you notice that it's getting progressively harder to get started (i.e., you're procrastinating), then either reduce the number of habits or ask yourself *why* you want to skip a day. The more you understand about your lack of motivation, the easier it will be to overcome it.

13. Build one routine at a time, because each new routine increases the difficulty of sticking with your current habits. Only when *you* feel that a stack has become a permanent behavior should you consider adding a new routine.

That's it—thirteen steps to build a stack that will help you overcome the daily challenge of procrastination. I won't lie and say it'll be easy 100% of the time, but if you stick to these steps, then you can overcome any challenge that comes your way.

Activity #4: Challenge Your Daily Procrastination Tendencies

Even the most productive people occasionally struggle with the urge to skip certain tasks. This is especially true if you're not looking forward to something. That's why I recommend using the following six practices whenever you feel that day-to-day urge to procrastinate:

1. Set aside five minutes to evaluate any potential emergency that pops up during your day. Think of the worst-case scenario if you ignore it. If there's even a *small chance* that it could have a disastrous outcome, then drop what you're doing and take the first step to resolve the issue.

2. Use the Eisenhower Matrix to make quick decisions about every new request for your time. Get in the practice of evaluating all your tasks using the matrix's four quadrants, which will help you recognize what's truly important for your personal and professional life.

3. Build the discomfort habit if you keep putting off challenging tasks because they're not as enjoyable as your hobbies or the other ways you pass time.

4. Use the awareness habit to identify the signs of when you're about to procrastinate on a task. Keep track of the times you do this daily, so you can recognize what triggers your desire to put off certain activities.

5. Use temptation bundling to create rules where you're allowed to engage in an enjoyable experience only when you complete an action that benefits you in the long term.

137

6. Attach all tasks to a goal by making a list of your personal and professional responsibilities, then connecting each to an important value or goal.

There you have it—four activities that can help you turn all the information you've learned into a simple action plan. I challenge you to set aside 30–60 minutes each day for the next week to implement the one-time tasks. After that, I urge you to build the habits that I just mentioned into your daily routine.

If you add this framework to your life, you'll discover that it's not hard to face procrastination head on and take positive action on the difficult tasks in your life.

FINAL THOUGHTS ON *HOW TO STOP PROCRASTINATING*

Well, we've reached the end of *How to Stop Procrastinating*. You now know what it takes to eliminate the bad habit of procrastination and become someone who easily manages all those challenging day-to-day activities.

On the surface, procrastination might not seem like a big deal. But if you allow it to go unchecked, there might be a day where this bad habit will create a very serious, negative consequence. It could cause you to miss an important medical diagnosis. Or to pay a "stupidity tax" like yours truly. Or to not talk to someone who needs help.

The good news is procrastination doesn't have to control your life. You now have a framework in which you will never allow those important tasks and activities to slip through the cracks.

Now it's up to you.

As we close this discussion, I urge you to overcome that *resistance* all readers have whenever they complete a book. In other words, instead of finishing this book, leaving a positive review on Amazon (hint, hint), and moving on to the next title, I recommend *implementing* what you've just learned.

You can take that first step by completing the four activities we just covered. Schedule those one-time exercises on your calendar, make that commitment to do a weekly review, and then build that daily habit stack to prevent your procrastination tendencies.

When you focus on what's important in life and only complete the tasks related to these goals (and nothing else), your problems stemming from procrastination will go away.

Sure, there will be times when you backslide. Occasionally, you will fail to complete the tasks that you've scheduled for that day. But remind yourself that it's okay to fail and make mistakes. Just stick to the game plan! Remember: perseverance is one of the true "secrets" to success.

Simply focus on making small improvements every day. Celebrate each victory. And get excited about how you're finally overcoming a bad habit that often holds people back from achieving their goals.

I wish you the best of luck.

—Steve "S.J." Scott

ONE LAST REMINDER . . .

We've covered a wealth of information in this book, but that doesn't mean your self-educational efforts should end here. In fact, I've created a small companion website that includes many resources mentioned throughout *How to Stop Procrastinating*.

Here are just a few things I've included:

» *How to Stop Procrastinating Quick Start Guide*, which is a printable reference guide of all the exercises, checklists, and action items included in this book.

» Each link and resource mentioned in this book.

» A visual walk-through of my weekly calendar, which shows how I specifically use the time blocking technique.

» The Todoist walk-through video.

» The Evernote walk-through video.

» A printable download that you can use to implement the Eisenhower Matrix.

» The complete 13-step process of how to build a habit-stacking routine.

Plus, I will be adding more goodies to this website in the months to come. So, if you're interested in expanding on what you've learned in this book, then click this link and join us today:

www.developgoodhabits.com/procrastination-website

THANK YOU!

Before you go, we'd like to say thank you for purchasing my book.

You could have picked from dozens of books on habit development, but you took a chance and checked out this one.

So, big thanks for downloading this book and reading all the way to the end.

Now we'd like ask for a small favor. **Could you please take a minute or two and leave a review for this book on Amazon?**

This feedback will help us continue to write the kind of Kindle books that help you get results. And if you loved it, please let us know.

MORE BOOKS BY STEVE

» *Habit Stacking: 127 Small Changes to Improve Your Health, Wealth, and Happiness*

» *Novice to Expert: 6 Steps to Learn Anything, Increase Your Knowledge, and Master New Skills*

» *Declutter Your Mind: How to Stop Worrying, Relieve Anxiety, and Eliminate Negative Thinking*

» *The Miracle Morning for Writers: How to Build a Writing Ritual That Increases Your Impact and Your Income*

» *10-Minute Digital Declutter: The Simple Habit to Eliminate Technology Overload*

» *10-Minute Declutter: The Stress-Free Habit for Simplifying Your Home*

» *The Accountability Manifesto: How Accountability Helps You Stick to Goals*

» *Confident You: An Introvert's Guide to Success in Life and Business*

» *Exercise Every Day: 32 Tactics for Building the Exercise Habit (Even If You Hate Working Out)*

» *The Daily Entrepreneur: 33 Success Habits for Small Business Owners, Freelancers and Aspiring 9-to-5 Escape Artists*

» *Master Evernote: The Unofficial Guide to Organizing Your Life with Evernote (Plus 75 Ideas for Getting Started)*

» *Bad Habits No More: 25 Steps to Break Any Bad Habit*

» *To-Do List Makeover: A Simple Guide to Getting the Important Things Done*

» *23 Anti-Procrastination Habits: How to Stop Being Lazy and Get Results in Your Life*

» *S.M.A.R.T. Goals Made Simple: 10 Steps to Master Your Personal and Career Goals*

» *115 Productivity Apps to Maximize Your Time: Apps for iPhone, iPad, Android, Kindle Fire and PC/iOS Desktop Computers*

» *Writing Habit Mastery: How to Write 2,000 Words a Day and Forever Cure Writer's Block*

» *Daily Inbox Zero: 9 Proven Steps to Eliminate Email Overload*

» *Wake Up Successful: How to Increase Your Energy and Achieve Any Goal with a Morning Routine*

» *10,000 Steps Blueprint: The Daily Walking Habit for Healthy Weight Loss and Lifelong Fitness*

» *70 Healthy Habits: How to Eat Better, Feel Great, Get More Energy and Live a Healthy Lifestyle*

» *Resolutions That Stick! How 12 Habits Can Transform Your New Year*